WHAT I
SAYING ABOUT *RESILIENT* . . .

Dr. Craig Oliver is a true guide and proven leader on the road to resilience. Let this resource—practical, powerful, biblical and bold—add steel to your soul.

Will Mancini
Author of *Future Church* and Founder of The Future
    Church Company
Houston, Texas

I once heard that the secret to being relevant is found within a few rules: be authentic, be empathetic, and always take action. If this is true, it authenticates the brilliance of Dr. Craig L. Oliver, Sr. Over the last twenty years, he has embodied these three rules with precision. Those who read *Resilient* will borrow the author's mindset and leap one step closer to destiny. This no-holds-barred, no-excuses approach is just what the doctor ordered.

Pastor Keion D. Henderson
Senior Pastor of the Lighthouse Church
Houston, Texas

If ever there was a time that the world needs to hear a message of strength, hope, and perseverance, it is now. In his book, *Resilient*, Dr. Craig L. Oliver, Sr., presents a timely and biblically sound message to encourage the heart and strengthen the resolve of all who read it. Dr. Oliver skillfully takes the reader on a transparent journey filled with peaks and valleys, trusting in God's power to provide the grace to be resilient through it all. I highly recommend this book as an essential resource in the lives of believers across the world.

> **Bishop Paul S. Morton, Sr.**
> **Founder of Full Gospel Baptist Church Fellowship International**
> **Overseer of Changing A Generation Ministries,**
>   **Atlanta, Georgia**
> **Overseer of Greater St. Stephen Ministries,**
>   **New Orleans, Louisiana**

In *Resilient*, Dr. Craig Oliver shares from the timeless Word of God and the well of life's experiences to provide the reader with a practical guide to jumping back to one's God-assigned position in Christ even when faced with the challenges of contemporary life. Everyone who struggles with regaining their footing and identity in Christ should read this insightful book. It is a light in the darkness of misaligned destinies.

> **Dr. Robert Smith, Jr.**
> **Charles T. Carter Baptist Chair of Divinity at**
>   **Beeson Divinity School**
> **Samford University, Homewood, Alabama**

Resilient is an on-time message, and my good friend, Dr. Craig Oliver, is an on-time messenger. With great sensitivity to human challenges as well as divine oversight, he weaves a rich tapestry of how you are actually more resilient, by God's grace, than you realize. This book will give you overdoses of encouragement and point you to the ever-present strength of God. This message won't end with you—you'll share it with everyone you love.

> **Sam Chand**
> **Church Consultant, Leadership Architect,**
>   **and Author of *Leadership Pain***
> **Atlanta, Georgia**

Dr. Craig Oliver is one of the best communicators in our lifetime. In his book, *Resilient*, he skillfully unveils how resilience is much more than merely not quitting—it's the capacity to adapt to adversity, trauma, disasters, and trouble of any kind. When we experience setbacks and heartaches, Dr. Oliver guides us in very practical ways to steward what God has entrusted to us in the midst of our difficulties. This powerful book will change your life and grow your organization.

Dr. Robert J. Watkins
CEO of Conquer Worldwide
Orlando, Florida

Dr. Craig Oliver is an extraordinary leader, a visionary pastor, and an unforgettable communicator. He has written an instant classic that will transform your life and open your eyes to the power of resilience in your life. "Resilient" is the perfect word to describe this incredible book—it encourages you, strengthens you and challenges you. Everyone should grab this book to be reminded of how God works in our lives through challenging seasons and grows us in immeasurable ways.

Bryan Carter
Senior Pastor of Concord Church and author of _Made to Last_
Dallas, Texas

Craig Oliver is a clarion voice amidst the clamoring noise of our day. He is a leader's leader, an adventurer's guide, and a physician's doctor. In _Resilient_, Dr. Oliver provides a poignant picture of how to meet God in our suffering as we build a bridge from our past to our future. On this journey you won't find false hope or faulty promises. Instead, you'll find the power of God to build you into the kind of person who can live into your divine destiny. If you are a leader (or you want to be a leader but feel trapped in your past or are simply having trouble seeing God's hand in the midst of your pain), I invite you to read this book because Dr. Oliver will help you cross the bridge to your purpose.

Dave Rhodes
Co-founder of the Future Church Company, Strategic Director
of the Grace Family of Churches, and Author of _Redefining_
Normal
Atlanta, Georgia

This book is filled with inspiring personal stories, practical wisdom, and theological depth. Like a skilled doctor, Dr. Oliver identifies barriers that keep us from living a resilient life and directs his readers to God's amazing LOVE and grace. If you're ready to live a resilient life of faith, this book is a must-read.

Dr. Letra Smith
Elizabeth Baptist Church Missions/Discipleship Director or
** Christian Education Director**
Atlanta, Georgia

RESILIENT

RESILIENT

Building a bridge to strength, wisdom, and hope

CRAIG L. OLIVER

ISBNs:
Print: 978-1-951022-20-4
Ebook versions: 978-1-951022-21-1

Cover design and interior formatting by Anne McLaughlin, Blue Lake Design
Published by Craig L. Oliver Ministries

Printed in the United States

This book is dedicated to the incredible members of Elizabeth Baptist Church, people who have endured burdens that have tested their resilience. As your pastor, I have wept with you as you've faced unimaginable personal pain, tragic loss, economic struggles, and more recently, disorientation and disruption during the pandemic. And yet, as a community, I trust that we will continue in our resilient walk of faith in discovering the strength, wisdom, and hope found in God and his Word.

And to you, dear reader, I dedicate this book as well. Even if you don't know me personally, I hope you sense my heart as you read these pages. You'll see that we share some things in common—the pains and pressures of life, as well as plenty of God's blessings. All of us face heartaches and detours on our journeys, and in those moments of confusion and doubt, we can cling to God's truth and experience his grace, living with resilience as we dare to walk this bridge plank by plank.

CONTENTS

Foreword 13

Introduction 15

Chapter 1 Realistic about Everything. .21

Chapter 2 Experiencing God 43

Chapter 3 Steadfast Hope 61

Chapter 4 Intervention from God. 83

Chapter 5 Look at Your Story 99

Chapter 6 Imagine a Better Future 119

Chapter 7 Empowered by the Gospel. .139

Chapter 8 Network of Faith. 157

Chapter 9 Triumph through Christ 175

Endnotes 193

Acknowledgments 197

Using *Resilient* in Small Groups and Classes 199

About the Author. 203

Resources 205

FOREWORD

All of us have experienced difficult seasons that stretched our faith beyond anything we could have ever imagined. Resilience is very seldom revealed in good times. Our capacity to persevere is discovered only during the difficulties of life, and our true character is found in our ability to keep trusting in the promises of God. Edgar Guest captures this idea in the last stanza of his poem "See It Through."

> Even hope may seem but futile,
> When with troubles you're beset,
> But remember you are facing
> Just what other men have met.
> You may fail, but fall still fighting;
> Don't give up, whate'er you do;
> Eyes front, head high to the finish.
> See it through!

It may take years to fully understand the impact of the global pandemic. Many people became utterly exhausted, yet they kept fighting, loving, and serving. Our ability to be resilient is one of the most significant witnesses to our relationship with Christ. Sadly, I have talked to leaders from across the world who have contemplated walking away from their positions. They have been disillusioned and discouraged to the point of resignation. During this difficult season, I have often reminded people that the devil can never take from you what God has for you, but he can make it so complicated that you may surrender it yourself.

This spirit of resignation and surrender is running rampant today. Dr. Oliver is a world-renowned thought leader who has done excellent research in this area. His leadership transcends borders and focuses on the intersection of leadership and developmental strategies for individuals, families, teams, churches, businesses, and other organizations. If you are wondering how to press on, the message of this book is pivotal to your progress. I am confident that the hidden gems found in these pages will help you get over and get through any hurdle you face.

I have often wondered what the world would be like if we saved, stored, and used our resilience as outlined in this book. I believe that many dreams, goals, and desires would not lie dormant or stay in the stage of infancy. Instead, external circumstances could never completely deter us from reaching our goals. We all have had "comma moments" that caused us to pause; however, resilience gives us the strength to hit play again and persevere. Subsequently, everything God has called us to complete becomes an answer to the Kingdom equation that enables us to fulfill God's will for our lives.

For such a time as this, Dr. Craig Oliver masterfully penned this book to shed light on the significance of resilience and our need for it. So often, we are told that we should be resilient, but few have given us a workable strategy. Dr. Oliver offers practical steps that help all of us, regardless of where we are in our faith journey. I am confident that this book will inspire you and encourage you to persevere in your destiny.

Bishop Joseph W. Walker, III
Senior Pastor of Mt. Zion Baptist Church
Nashville, Tennessee

INTRODUCTION

The rain to the wind said,
"You push and I'll pelt."
They so smote the garden bed
That the flowers actually knelt,
And lay lodged—though not dead.
I know how the flowers felt.

—*Robert Frost*

Frost's poem expresses two truths: the hard reality of life and our resolve to be resilient. The flowers took a beating, but there was still life in them: "And lay lodged—though not dead." Is this not the attitude of resilient people? In our life's journey, we invariably encounter rough weather and torrents of rain that can devastate us. We experience sickness, heartbreak, and grief. We agonize through our children's growing pains. We feel the hurt of people we love. We run into seemingly intractable problems in our work. We despair at the gloomy and alarming newscasts.

Yes, there are those days when it seems the hard rain and the powerful winds have conspired against us, saying, "You push and I'll pelt," but thank God for the recurring realization that no night is forever, and no one sees a rainbow until they've had the rain.

I wish every heartache ended with blessings, but all of us can think of exceptions among our acquaintances—storm-swept souls who are blown into the rocky shallows of self-pity, and for some reason never seem to get out of it. But I'm convinced that's the exception.

I salute the resilient people I've known:

- Sick people, perhaps faced with an uncertain future but cheerfully engaged in a gallant struggle.

- Grieving people, stung by the death of one dearly cherished but facing the future with courage and hope.

- Working people, phased out of one job but training themselves for another.

- Single people, deprived of or uncoupled from a marriage but avoiding self-pity and building useful lives.

Stop to think about how many resilient people you are privileged to know.

As believers, resilience should be no stranger. If the faith has grasped us at all, we realize that we aren't alone. In fact, we are empowered and encouraged by One who is unconquerable. Of course, this doesn't mean that we're exempt from suffering or that we can fully explain all suffering, but it means that we have good reason to be resilient—because in Jesus Christ we have glimpsed enough of God to know that we never drift beyond the circle of his sufficient love and care that sustains us.

Paul's letter to the people of Corinth expresses resilient resolve: "We are afflicted in every way, but not crushed; perplexed, but not driven to despair; persecuted, but not forsaken; struck down, but not destroyed . . . so we do not lose heart" (2 Corinthians 4:8-9, 16).

Our resilience doesn't come from a hope that we'll escape suffering. Instead, it comes from the conviction that God, in his infinite wisdom and love, will weave even our deepest pain into a beautiful fabric of our lives. We may not get what we asked for, but God gives us something very different, something we may not have wanted, but something even more valuable. I've always appreciated the strong faith of the soldier who penned this prayer. It is more poignant because he was killed in battle not long after he wrote it.

I asked God for strength, that I might achieve.
I was made weak, that I might learn humbly to obey.
I asked for health, that I might do greater things.
I was given infirmity, that I might do better things.
I asked for riches, that I might be happy.
I was given poverty, that I might be wise.
I asked for power that I might have the praise of men.
I was given weakness, that I might feel the need of God.
I asked for all things, that I might enjoy life.
I was given life, that I might enjoy all things.
I got nothing that I asked for but got everything I had hoped for.
Almost despite myself, my unspoken prayers were answered.
I am, among all people, most richly blessed.

We thank God for giving us the resilient fiber in the human spirit, and by the power of God at work in us, it renews us and sets us on the high road once again.

I believe the common thread in the tapestry of faith is the dynamic spirit of resilience. Real resilience is always a derivative of faith. President Lincoln remarked, "I have been driven to my knees by the overwhelming conviction that I had nowhere else to go." We remember his comment to someone who claimed that God was on the side of the Union: "Sir, my concern is not whether God is on our side; my greatest concern is to be on God's side, for God is always right." That, I believe, is the key to resilience: to be on God's side, no matter what the circumstances may be.

In the recent past, we've suffered racial injustice and unrest, a global pandemic that has devastated families, economic difficulties, and a polarized society. It's easy to be overwhelmed with all of this, so we need to ask, "What has God given us so that we can be resilient in our faith, hope, and love?" During the lockdowns, we longed for things to "go back to normal," but for many people, normal will never return. Still, God promises to give us something better: a stronger faith, deeper love, and more focused hope. As we trust him, we'll have more integrity, we'll pursue justice and mercy, and God's grace will overflow into the lives of those around us. Through it all, we'll see that Jesus is worthy of our love and loyalty.

Each of us has a favorite verse or two in the Bible. If I were to choose five or six favorite verses, I would certainly include Paul's simple declaration, "And we know that for those who love God all things work together for good, for those who are called according to his purpose" (Romans 8:28).

What a promise to stand on! "All things" aren't inherently good in themselves, but God uses them for our good and his glory. To the degree that we believe this promise, we'll have steadfast faith that no matter what happens, we can trust that God is at work. In other words, we'll be resilient. We'll bounce back up when we fall, we'll be filled with the love of God when we're deflated, and we'll find Jesus to be our solid rock in the middle of the storm.

The metaphor of growing resilience is a bridge, but not one of steel—it's a rope bridge, one that we build carefully, adding one plank at a time. In each chapter, we'll add a new plank so we can take another step toward faith-filled tenacity.

As you begin this book, let me pray for you:

We acknowledge, our Father, that it sometimes feels like the storm is too much for us. We feel down and out, "afflicted, perplexed, persecuted, and struck down." Lead each of us in our pilgrimage of faith to that peak where we can also exclaim enthusiastically with Paul, "afflicted, yes, but not crushed; perplexed, yes, but not driven to despair; persecuted, yes, but not forsaken; struck down, yes, but not destroyed."

Move in our hearts, dear God. Renew our hearts with strengthening joy, a hopeful disposition, and enlightened eyes to behold the presence of Christ with us. Bind us more closely to each other and to him, and lift up our hearts and minds to you, Lord, that we may go out, renewed in body, soul, and spirit—nourished and made new.

We ask it in the name of Christ, whose eternal resilience is the guiding light for each of us. In his name, we pray. Amen.

CHAPTER 1

REALISTIC ABOUT EVERYTHING

A living faith is nothing else than a steadfast pursuit of God through all that disguises, disfigures, demolishes and seeks, so to speak, to abolish him.

—*Jean-Pierre de Caussade*

The first plank in the bridge is being *realistic*. We simply won't make progress in our faith journey if we insist on making excuses, rationalizing our choices, and living in denial. Objectivity is essential.

When our lives come unglued, we have the opportunity to see two very different realities: what is plainly obvious right in front of us . . . and the previously unseen purposes of God. The second reality is often hidden from us, but heartaches have a way of fine-tuning our senses so we notice it. I know, because I've been there.

When I'm speaking on Sunday mornings, some people may look at me and assume that I've never experienced a day of despair in my life. They would be wrong. The darkest, most difficult season of my life was when I endured a domestic difficulty that resulted in the dissolution of a union. In other words, my marriage disintegrated. Within the span of twenty-four months, I graduated from college, began my career as a pastor, got married, and we had a baby. The rapid series of changes created unbearable stress, and I didn't handle it well. I had a disastrous maturity deficit in both categories: marriage and ministry.

I'd like to blame my wife, but that would be neither true nor fair. Both of us share some of the responsibility for our troubles, but the lion's share was mine. When we filed for divorce, I believed I'd driven a nail in the coffin of my role as a pastor, and I was done with ministry. I wasn't the only one who came to that conclusion. A number of my peers and mentors were as useless as Job's friends. They told me, "Craig, you should just quit. Your life is over." Instead of a scarlet A, I was sure God had given me a scarlet L in his heavenly ledger book . . . L for loser. I looked for the nearest exit to get off the rocky highway I'd been on. I'd had such grand hopes and big dreams, but they were all shattered into tiny slivers.

I moved out of our house and rented an apartment, which felt more like a deep, dark dungeon. The months of conflict, resentment, self-doubt, and shame took a heavy toll, and on one particular day, the darkness enveloped me like a shroud. I was alone, I'd left my baby, and I was staring at the end of the only career I'd ever wanted. But that's not all—the year was 1999, and the news was filled with dire predictions about the catastrophe that would occur when the calendar turned to the year 2000: Y2K. (If you're too young to recall what that was like, ask your parents. They'll remember!) I was living alone with rented furniture and a television sitting on the box it had come in. I was almost certainly clinically depressed, but I heeded the warnings from the technology experts. I stocked up on canned goods so I could eat after the power grid collapsed and food shortages plagued the world, and I bought survival gear. The alarmists advised buying a gun with plenty of ammunition to defend against those who would take your food and supplies, so I got a license to carry and bought a 9mm Glock pistol.

I bought the Glock to protect myself from murderers, robbers, and vandals, but on that bleak day, I looked down the barrel and considered using it on myself. The enemy wasn't "out there," it was "in here" . . . to kill, steal, and destroy myself. My dreams had become nightmares, my hopes were swallowed in doubt, and my clear thinking had become muddled by fear-driven lies. I believed I had come to the end, and the pistol could free me from all the pain.

As I pointed the gun toward myself, I remembered something a seminary professor had told our class: "Suicide is a permanent solution to a temporary problem." Could she possibly be right? Was my current pit of despair only a temporary problem? It sure seemed permanent. Would I ever feel a sense of joy, hope, and delight again? It seemed unfathomable, but I decided to believe her. As I held the gun in my hand, I realized that a simple act of pointing and pulling the trigger would be a purchase I couldn't return. The sale would be final.

I put the gun down and reached for my Bible. I thought, *Maybe God will speak to me.* I flipped it open to 1 Kings 19 and read about the prophet Elijah. He had seen God do something amazing on Mt. Carmel when he challenged the prophets of Baal to call down fire from heaven to burn up a sacrifice. The pagan prophets chanted, cut themselves, and tried their best to induce their god to action, but the heavens were silent. Then Elijah prayed, and fire fell from heaven, consuming the sacrifice, the water in the trenches around it, and the altar itself! Surely, this would make Elijah bold and confident! But it didn't. Queen Jezebel threatened to kill him, and he ran like a scared little child.

Elijah got far away from the queen, and he prayed. His prayer wasn't for protection, and it wasn't for wisdom and strength. He asked God to be his accomplice in his suicide: "It is enough; now, O Lord, take away my life, for I am no better than my fathers" (1 Kings 19:4). But of course, God had other plans for his depressed prophet. God gave him a place to sleep, and then he sent an angel to provide nourishment. That wasn't enough to lift the gloom, however. Elijah traveled for forty days to Horeb, and when

God met him there, the prophet poured out a heart full of self-pity. God told him to stand in a cave on the mountain. He sent a strong wind like a tornado, but God wasn't in the wind. God caused the earth to shake, but he wasn't in the earthquake. A fire roared over the mountain, but God wasn't there either. Then, Elijah heard a whisper—it was the Lord! God patiently, lovingly entered into a dialogue with him, restored him to his mission, and assured him that he wasn't alone. There were still seven thousand faithful people in Israel!

In that precious moment, God was speaking directly to me. My career was, in a small way, parallel to Elijah's. God had used me to build our church and change lives, but I'd found myself in the pit of despair, exhausted mentally and physically, running and hiding, but willing to listen to God communicate his love for me. And today, as I write these words and you read them, this conversation wouldn't be taking place if God hadn't whispered to me when all I wanted to do was end it all. Please don't misunderstand: I'm not saying that God stepped in to radically change all the circumstances of my life at that moment, but he stepped in to stop a tragic decision, communicate his heart of compassion, and teach me that no one is immune from the ravages of doubt and depression. From that day forward, I've never looked at people who are hurting the same way. It used to be "them" . . . now it's "us."

> From that day forward, I've never looked at people who are hurting the same way. It used to be "them" . . . now it's "us."

GRIT, ENDURANCE, AND RESILIENCE

These three words overlap, and most of us use them interchangeably. It's instructive, though, to look under the hood to examine each one.

Grit

In her book, *Grit: The Power of Passion and Perseverance*, Angela Duckworth inspires people to be tenacious. She observes: "Optimists . . . are just as likely to encounter bad events as pessimists. Where they diverge is in their explanations: optimists habitually search for temporary and specific causes of their suffering, whereas pessimists assume permanent and pervasive causes are to blame."[1] You would think that those who are loved by the God of the universe, rescued from sin, death, and hell, and given a purpose to advance the greatest enterprise (the Great Commission) the world has ever known would be eternal optimists, but that's not always the case. Far too often, we lack grit, we aren't resilient, and we can't look reality in the eye because it's too discouraging.

Endurance

One of the most stirring stories in the modern world is the expedition of Ernest Shackleton and his crew to be the first to cross the continent of Antarctica by way of the South Pole. Their ship was aptly named *Endurance*, but it got stuck in the ice for almost a year, and on October 27, 1915, pressure from the icepack cracked the hull and allowed freezing water to flood the compartments where the men had been confined. The crew salvaged provisions from the ship and lived in tents on the ice. Shackleton commented, "There was no alternative but to camp once more on the floe and to possess our souls with what patience we could till conditions should appear more favorable for a renewal of the attempt to escape."[2]

The ice drifted northward until they sighted two islands in the distance. For months, they had carried and pushed small boats over the ice, and now they could use them. The seas were treacherous, but they made it to Elephant Island. They were finally on solid land, but they were marooned with no way to let anyone know where they were. Shackleton and five other men made the desperate decision to try to reach a whaling station on South Georgia Island . . . 800 miles away. For sixteen days, they navigated one of the little boats through furious winds and 100-foot waves. "Every surge of the sea was an enemy to be watched and circumvented. The wind simply shrieked as it tore the tops off the waves. Down into the valleys, up to tossing heights, straining until her seams opened, swung our little boat."

In one of the greatest feats of navigation, Shackleton and his crew of five found the island, which is no more than a dot in the vast South Atlantic Ocean. The storm was so fierce that they had to land on the opposite side of the island, so for thirty-six hours, Shackleton and two other men hiked over the mountains and slid down glaciers. Finally, they staggered into the little village with "their hair and beards stringy and matted, their faces blackened with soot from blubber stoves and creased from nearly two years of stress and privation."

A whaler looked at these men and asked, "Who the hell are you?"

The exhausted, soot-covered man in the middle said, "My name is Shackleton."

The whaler, hardened by years of brutal work, was stunned. He turned away and wept. The men immediately sent a rescue party to the other side of the island to pick up the three who had remained with their little boat. Then Shackleton and the whalers mounted a massive effort to return to Elephant Island for the twenty-two men who had been surviving on penguin meat for many weeks. Shackleton exhibited supreme courage in the face of phenomenal dangers and setbacks. His endurance has inspired generations of people who have heard his story.[3]

Resilience

Let's look at the root of two important words. The word *resilience* comes from the Latin *resilire*, combining *re-* ("back") and *salire* ("to jump, leap") to mean "to rebound or recoil"—in other words, to jump back or snap back. Resilience is the ability to cope with, overcome, and grow mentally, physically, or spiritually in the face of adversity. The word *adversity* comes from the Latin *adversus*: "turned against." It is a state of hardship, affliction, or misfortune. Those with resilience find truth in Nietzsche's saying, "If it doesn't destroy us, it makes us stronger." Every difficulty we overcome and every victory we win increases our resilience, providing confidence that we can grow as we face the next adversity.

Resilience isn't the ability to avoid trouble; it's the capacity to adapt to adversity, trauma, disasters, and trouble of any kind. It's the ability to bounce back, to recover, to get back on your feet after a fall. It's like a rubber band that is stretched to its limit but returns to its normal size and shape when the pressure is released.[4] In the Scriptures, resilience is often linked to hope. No matter how bleak things look, we have the assurance that God hasn't forgotten us, he hasn't lost control of the universe, and he has something magnificent for us. One of my favorite passages is in Paul's second letter to the Corinthians. The people in that church had a lot of problems—and in fact, they caused most of them! Paul encouraged them to be realistic about their flaws and their weaknesses. After he explained that God has given us the treasure of the gospel of grace, he reminds them, "But we have this treasure in jars of clay, to show that the surpassing power belongs to God and not to us" (2 Corinthians 4:7). We aren't exempt from suffering, but Paul assures us that God will never waste our pain.

> Resilience isn't the ability to avoid trouble; it's the capacity to adapt to adversity, trauma, disasters, and trouble of any kind.

Paul acknowledged that we can get so discouraged that we want to give up, or in his words, "lose heart." He assured them (and us): "So we do not lose heart. Though our outer self is wasting away, our inner self is being renewed day by day. For this light momentary affliction is preparing for us an eternal weight of glory beyond all comparison, as we look not to the things that are seen but to the things that are unseen. For the things that are seen are transient, but the things that are unseen are eternal" (vv. 16-18). Paul is saying, "Sure, life can be hard . . . really hard. Our faith can waver, our confidence can wane, and our health can deteriorate. That's why we need to know—beyond a shadow of a doubt—that God is doing something so wonderful that we can't even imagine it. We may not experience the blessing soon, or even in this life, but we have assurance that someday we'll enjoy "an eternal weight of glory beyond all comparison." This is the assurance that gives us strength . . . it's what makes us resilient.

There is, in my opinion, no better example of godly resilience than Martin Luther King, Jr. For years, he spoke truth to power and advocated the astonishing strategy of nonviolence in combating racism. He was fiercely opposed, falsely accused, physically attacked, and bitterly condemned, but he never stopped. He received many death threats and several assassination attempts, until one of those attempts proved fatal. Among his many powerful quotes are these:

- "I believe that unarmed truth and unconditional love will have the final word in reality. This is why right, temporarily defeated, is stronger than evil triumphant."

- "There comes a time when one must take a position that is neither safe, nor politic, nor popular, but he must take it because conscience tells him it is right."

- "We must accept finite disappointment, but never lose infinite hope."

✦ "Forgiveness is not an occasional act. It is a permanent attitude."[5]

I believe he would tell us today, "Stay in the fight, be resilient in love, and be a source of light to everyone around you."

THE BRIDGE

Let me give you a heads-up about where we're going. To keep us focused on the concepts that make us steadfast and immovable in our faith, I'm using the word *resilient* as an acrostic in the chapter titles:

Realistic about Everything
Experiencing God
Steadfast in Hope
Intervention from God
Look at Your Story
Imagine a Better Future
Empowered by the Gospel
Network of Faith
Triumph through Christ

As I've said, a bridge is a perfect metaphor for our journey of resilience. We often think of the Golden Gate Bridge in San Francisco, the Mackinac Bridge in Michigan, or the Sunshine Skyway Bridge in my hometown of St. Petersburg. These are engineering marvels, but the bridges we cross in our spiritual journeys are more tenuous and require more attention as we make our way across them—more like a rope bridge. Each of the elements of resilience is a plank in the bridge that takes us from *problematic adversity* to *positive adjustments*. And like any bridge, each component of the structure is crucial—we need them all to make it to our desired destination.

MISGUIDED CONCLUSIONS

When I felt shaken as a young leader and wanted to end it all, and even now sometimes when I'm on the verge of losing heart, it's because I've come to the conclusion that "Life isn't fair," "I don't deserve this," and "Things are completely out of control." I look around at the lives of others and want to bark at God, "Why do things work out for them but not for me?"

All of us have these feelings and thoughts from time to time. It's part of being human, but some of us have turned these complaints into a way of life! We worry, and we want people to know how much we worry. We wear it like a badge of honor! But worry isn't one of the fruit of the Spirit. Concern makes us alert and proactive, but worry is the conclusion that I know better than God how my life ought to go.

We live in a culture that makes grand promises, and unfortunately, we believe them! Every commercial on television, every billboard, and every magazine ad promises the product or service will make us rich, beautiful, and happy. Don't believe me? Look again. The toothpaste ads don't just say the white paste will make your teeth clean. The promise is that your pearly white teeth will make you gorgeous and popular! The investment company ads promise to make your life full of all the good things, including houses, boats, and vacations. And the beer commercials . . . don't get me started!

My point is that we're swimming upstream against the powerful current of our culture. We're bombarded by messages that tell us we deserve "the good life," which means freedom from pain and escape from any inconvenience. People who believe these subtle but effective lies often feel that God owes them happiness, and when suffering comes, they complain and collapse.

A clear-eyed view of reality and a hearty skepticism as we look at commercials and ads are essential if we're going to be resilient. Many

Christians believe God has promised them a life that's pleasant, perfect, and pristine, but that's not the message I read in the Bible. He has, indeed, given us "precious and magnificent promises" (2 Peter 1:4), but they are for purpose, power, and perseverance. Some churches preach a gospel that has been sterilized from suffering, but all we need to do is look at the life of Christ, Paul, the prophets, and all the heroes listed in Hebrews 11 to see that every person God uses has gone through severe difficulties. In fact, theologian A. W. Tozer commented, "It is doubtful whether God can bless a man [or woman] greatly until he has hurt him deeply."[6] So . . . this begs the question: Do we want God's agenda, purpose, and impact for our lives, or do we prefer personal peace and affluence above all else? The answer to this question determines the level of our resilience in times of trouble.

Make no mistake: the default setting of the human heart is to escape suffering and resist the training ground of hardships. We may use busyness to avoid the uncomfortable feelings, we may use substances to numb the pain, or we may mask our pain behind a veneer of toughness. These strategies, though, don't lead to hope, compassion, and, eventually, greater joy. In fact, they inevitably produce soul-killing self-pity and resentment. We always have a choice of how we respond, and our choice always has a dramatic impact on us and those who are close to us.

Is it possible to hope too much, to expect too much from God? Yes, let me explain. When we hope that God will bail us out of every difficulty, free us from every stress, and make our lives comfortable, we're on a collision course with reality! In his classic book, *Knowing God*, author and professor J. I. Packer explains how God uses our struggles to reveal more of his grace:

> This is what all the work of grace aims at—an ever deeper knowledge of God, and an ever closer fellowship with Him. Grace is God drawing us sinners closer and closer to Himself.

How does God in grace prosecute this purpose? Not by shielding us from assault by the world, the flesh, and the devil, nor by protecting us from burdensome and frustrating circumstances, nor yet by shielding us from troubles created by our own temperament and psychology; but rather by exposing us to all these things, so as to overwhelm us with a sense of our own inadequacy, and to drive us to cling to Him more closely. This is the ultimate reason, from our standpoint, why God fills our lives with troubles and perplexities of one sort and another—it is to ensure that we shall learn to hold Him fast.[7]

> God never wastes our pain. He will always use our suffering redemptively to *refine* us, *restore* us, *renew* our commitment to his purposes, and he will *recycle* our dreams to be more focused on him.

God never wastes our pain. He will always use our suffering redemptively to *refine* us, *restore* us, *renew* our commitment to his purposes, and he will *recycle* our dreams to be more focused on him. Initially, suffering causes us to look inward and wish for instant relief, but when we get on God's wavelength, we realize he has called us to be conduits of blessing rather than cisterns—we become open channels to pour God's love into others instead of being satisfied with only our own experience of his grace. We're rivers, not reservoirs.

As our hearts are more in tune with God in our times of difficulty, we'll see that our suffering is both transformational and transactional. We're transformed in our attitudes and responses, and God uses us to care for people we might have overlooked before.

THE UNIVERSITY OF ADVERSITY

Some experts say that resilience is developed, and others insist it's discovered inside us. I believe it's a bit of both, but I'm not sure it matters, just so it appears when we need it most. Either way, resilience is a muscle that grows through exercise. When we lift weights, it feels like our muscles are getting weaker, but in fact, they're getting stronger. At the end of our reps, we're straining to do one more. It's far harder than the first few, but we get the greatest benefit out of our exercise at the outer limit of our endurance. That's where strength is developed. Resistance is absolutely necessary in the creation of resilience.

Like everyone, I've had to overcome resistance in many areas of my life. I have two undergraduate degrees, three master's degrees, and a Doctor of Divinity. I report these accomplishments, not to brag, but to recall a time when this level of education would have seemed utterly inconceivable to one of my previous teachers. A grammar school teacher, Mrs. Bash (an appropriate name, I thought), labeled me a "slow learner" and recommended that I be placed in a remedial class. My mother refused to believe Mrs. Bash's assessment. She marched down to Lynch Elementary School (another unfortunate and ironic name) and challenged my new placement. My mother's fierce but loving defiance was a model to me then, and it remains a model to me now: facing resistance with bold courage is essential if we're going to grow. Jazz poet Langston Hughes said, "Life for me ain't been no crystal stair." That's my story, too.

Adversity is the best school (I would argue, the only school) that teaches us the most important lessons in life. Great people almost invariably have endured great heartaches, but instead of letting their troubles crush them, the difficulties became rocket fuel for their advancement. In the spiritual world, we, like Elijah, get a clearer glimpse of God in our times of hardship. Corrie ten Boom survived a Nazi death camp in World War II, watching as her sister Betsie succumbed to starvation and disease.

Corrie's faith grew even from this horror. She later remarked, "There is no pit so deep that God's love is not deeper still."

We see this principle in the lives of courageous, compassionate people in every walk of life. Let me give three examples from the Scriptures.

Joseph

Joseph is perhaps the most complete and poignant Old Testament example of resilience. He was his father's favorite among the twelve sons, and they hated him for it. When his dad sent him to check on their work (Not a good idea at all! What was he thinking?), the brothers saw their chance to get rid of Joseph for good. Some of them planned to kill him, but others wanted to sell him as a slave to a passing caravan. They sold him into slavery and dipped his prized coat in sheep's blood so they could show it to their father and tell him that Joseph had been killed by wild animals.

The caravan took Joseph to Egypt where he was sold to Potiphar, a government official. Joseph proved to be invaluable to his owner, but Potiphar's wife had other ideas for his employment. When he refused her advances, she accused him of a sexual assault. My guess is that Potiphar knew the truth, so instead of having Joseph executed, he had him thrown in prison. There, Joseph remained for many years. During that time, the jailer realized Joseph was a supremely talented man, so he put him in charge of the prison. To Joseph, this must have seemed like the end game of his life, but God had other plans. Through a series of dreams he interpreted, the Pharoah was so impressed that he made Joseph the prime minister of the most powerful country on earth. In that role, he oversaw the collection and storage of food during seven years of harvest so the people could survive the coming seven years of drought. Miles away, Joseph's family suffered during the famine. When their father sent some of his brothers to buy food in Egypt, Joseph met them, but they didn't recognize him. He tested them to see if they had changed over the years, and only when he was convinced their hearts had softened did he announce that he was their brother.

What happened to Joseph during all that time as a slave and prisoner in Egypt? Suffering changed him. When he lived in his father's tent, he was a spoiled kid. Favoritism poisoned all the relationships in the family, and Joseph didn't have the wisdom to realize how his brothers would respond when he showed up to give their father a report on them. But during those long years in a foreign land, Joseph matured, and he found the grace to forgive his brothers. When their father died, they were afraid he would take revenge for their betrayal so many years before, but Joseph responded, "Do not fear, for am I in the place of God? As for you, you meant evil against me, but God meant it for good, to bring it about that many people should be kept alive, as they are today. So do not fear; I will provide for you and your little ones" (Genesis 50:19-21).

Joseph didn't say, "Oh, it didn't matter that you sold me as a slave." He didn't tell them, "It wasn't that bad. In prison I got three squares a day." And he didn't shrug and say, "I don't even know what you're talking about." Joseph lived in the middle of reality: their actions were evil . . . no doubt about it. But God used even their sins to put Joseph in a position to rescue the entire nation of Egypt from famine . . . and rescue his family, too. He had attended long classes in the university of adversity, and he graduated at the top of his class!

David

The biblical account of David is one of the most comprehensive biographies in the Bible, but I want to look particularly at two verses in one of his psalms. He wrote, "It is good for me that I was afflicted." We read that and recoil, "What! That doesn't make any sense at all. Affliction is anything but good!" But the verse continues: ". . . that I might learn your statutes" (Psalm 119:71). How do we get in touch with God's heart and his purposes? By learning the lessons only suffering can teach.

Despair occurs when our level of anxiety (or despair or fear or outrage) rises above our level of hope. It can happen when:

. . . we're blown off course by a cataclysmic event like a death, divorce, a layoff, disease, or abuse.

. . . we've made some really bad decisions that have created havoc for us and those we love.

. . . someone else has failed badly and we're stuck in the backwash of their chaos.

. . . natural catastrophes destroy our sense of normalcy.

. . . a pandemic upends everything.

Have any of these ever happened to you? Of course they have. They're entirely *normal* as part of the human condition. But also, they're *necessary* coursework to infuse God's most important lessons into us. In the same psalm, David reflected on the value of suffering: "Before I was afflicted I went astray, but now I keep your word" (Psalm 119:67). Is that the beneficial product of affliction in our lives? It can be.

Peter

We usually think of Peter's major blunder after Jesus' arrest when he denied that he even knew Jesus, but Jesus graciously restored the discouraged fisherman at an outdoor breakfast on the shores of Galilee. (Much more on this story later in the book.) After his colossal failure and Christ's forgiveness, Peter had a very different perspective.

For three years, Peter had expected Jesus to be the kind of Messiah he was looking for—a military/political leader who would lead a rebellion to conquer the Romans and kick them out of Palestine. When Jesus told the disciples that he was going to suffer and die, Peter couldn't imagine a dead

Messiah! He tried to correct Jesus (which never turns out well). But after Jesus ascended to the right hand of the Father, Peter finally realized that God's kingdom is very different than the one he had envisioned—it's one that is born in suffering, paradoxically thrives in suffering, and advances through suffering. We get a powerful insight into Peter's new perspective in his first letter. First, he points to the greatness of the gospel of grace:

> Blessed be the God and Father of our Lord Jesus Christ! According to his great mercy, he has caused us to be born again to a living hope through the resurrection of Jesus Christ from the dead, to an inheritance that is imperishable, undefiled, and unfading, kept in heaven for you, who by God's power are being guarded through faith for a salvation ready to be revealed in the last time. (1 Peter 1:3-5)

Then, he explains that the suffering they're experiencing as exiles isn't something outside of God's plans. In fact, God has specific purposes for their troubles:

> In this you rejoice, though now for a little while, if necessary, you have been grieved by various trials, so that the tested genuineness of your faith—more precious than gold that perishes though it is tested by fire—may be found to result in praise and glory and honor at the revelation of Jesus Christ. Though you have not seen him, you love him. Though you do not now see him, you believe in him and rejoice with joy that is inexpressible and filled with glory, obtaining the outcome of your faith, the salvation of your souls. (vv. 6-9)

Isn't that the kind of faith you long for? Isn't that the resilience you need? Our hope isn't that God will bail us out and make our lives easy, comfortable, and pleasant. No, our strong confidence is that God has eternal purposes that can only be realized through our suffering. In our struggles:

- God *prunes* us. We realize some of the things that mean so much to us have been hindrances to our relationship with God and our connections with people. When gardeners prune a grapevine, it looks drastic, but it's the way to have a healthy plant and an abundance of fruit. That's God's intention for our suffering, too.

- God *prepares* us. Training courses are the path to acquire and hone our skills in every field of endeavor. Why would we think spiritual life is different? From the day we trust in the matchless grace of God and are born again, we're in training to be who he wants us to be and do what he gives us to do.

- God *proves* us. When we go through difficulties, the pain reveals what's in our hearts. A racetrack is a proving ground for a car to show what it can do. When we're on the proving ground of heartaches, we're showing ourselves how much we've grown, and we're showing others that they can trust us.

MY HOPE FOR YOU

As I'm sure you can tell, the message of this book is very close to my heart. Like all of the most important lessons I've learned, this one is hard-won and deeply treasured. Walking with God isn't a straight line "up and to the right" on a graph. He leads us to mountaintops, for sure, but he also leads us into valleys, swamps, and dead ends. In each moment, he is good, he has a plan, and he is faithful. The social sciences have their theories of what makes people resilient. Certainly, support systems, self-awareness, right thinking, and compassion are important, but God has made us so that only he can fill the deepest hole in our hearts, strengthen us where we've been weak, and marvelously transform us into the likeness of Jesus. That process always—yes, always—involves suffering.

My hope, my reason for writing this book, is that God will give you a deeper grasp of his purposes in your pain. He occasionally provides quick relief, but far more often, he uses our headaches and heartaches as a class-room to teach us the most valuable lessons we'll ever learn.

Suffering doesn't mean that God doesn't care; it means that God cares about far more than our pleasure. He hasn't abandoned us; if any-thing, he uses our pain to draw us closer than ever.

I hope you'll give yourself permission to embark on the journey of walking with God through pain and suffering. Being realistic is essential, even though it's often uncomfortable to face the fact that God seldom provides instant and complete relief. In this process, you'll almost cer-tainly develop a deeper, richer relationship with him. Instead of trying to push painful emotions down so you don't feel them, you can embrace the tears, anger, and fear.

Being strong in faith doesn't mean our emotions are always pure and perfect. Quite the opposite. A strong faith gives us a firm foundation so we can be completely honest with God about the full range of our emotions, thoughts, and desires. King David prayed, "When I am afraid, I put my trust in you" (Psalm 56:3). He was honest about his fear, but his fear didn't obliterate his confidence that God was near, wise, kind, and loving. In fact, his honesty brought him closer to God.

> A strong faith gives us a firm foundation so we can be completely honest with God about the full range of our emotions, thoughts, and desires.

I hope God will give you new eyes as you read the Bible. You'll see that half of the psalms are laments, an entire book is called Lamentations, Jesus was the Suffering Servant, and all the heroes of the faith suffered but were resilient.

Don't you want to have a more realistic view of God and his purposes? Don't you want to develop godly resilience as you face hard times? Isn't that why you picked up this book?

At the end of each chapter, you'll find some questions to stimulate personal reflection and provide content for discussions with your spouse, friends, or small group. Take your time as you answer them, and ask God to speak to your heart. You'll also find an affirmation. Write it down, keep it with you, memorize it, and let God make it real in your life.

THINK ABOUT IT:

1. When have you come close to giving up . . . on yourself, on God, or on life? What were the circumstances? Why did you keep going?

2. How would you define and describe *resilience*? Who is someone you know who exemplifies this quality? What impact does that person have on you and others?

3. Do you agree or disagree that a misguided view of suffering always leads to self-pity and bitterness? Explain your answer.

4. Are you enrolled in the university of adversity, or are you skipping classes? How can you tell?

5. What are some ways God uses suffering to prune us, prepare us, and prove us?

6. What do you hope to get out of this book?

Affirmation:

Suffering doesn't mean that God doesn't care; it means that God cares about far more than our pleasure.

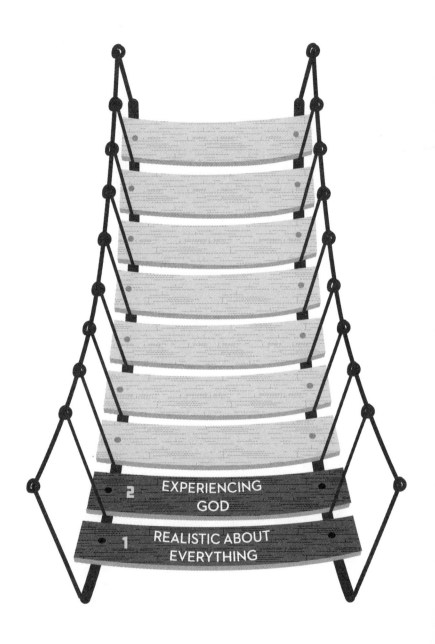

CHAPTER 2

EXPERIENCING GOD

To live by grace means to acknowledge my whole life story, the light side and the dark. In admitting my shadow side, I learn who I am and what God's grace means.

— *Brennan Manning*

With God, all things are possible; without him, nothing works and nothing matters. The second plank in your bridge to resilience is *experiencing God*.

Years ago, a speaker came to our church to teach in a women's conference. Near the end of the event, she announced to the audience, "The Lord just spoke to me and told me that someone here is being healed from cancer right now. If anyone has cancer, come down to the front, and I'll pray for you."

A number of women got up and walked toward her. The speaker prayed for God's healing, and then she told them, "I want you to make an appointment to see your doctor tomorrow so he can confirm that you are, indeed, healed. Then, come and tell Pastor Oliver your good news!"

A couple of weeks later on a Sunday, I preached, and after speaking to many people after the service, I went to my office. My phone rang. A security officer told me, "Pastor, Sister Maddie is here in the reception area, and she said she's not going to leave until she speaks to you."

I had no idea what this was about, so as I walked out of my office and down the hall to meet her, I braced myself for whatever was coming.

I said, "Hello, Sister Maddie, how are you?"

"Not well," she answered sullenly.

"What's going on? How can I help you?"

"I'm sure you know, Pastor, that the speaker at the women's conference said that God was going to heal us of cancer, and she told us to see our doctor to confirm the miracle." The look on her face told me where this conversation was headed. She took a deep breath and told me, "I made an appointment with my doctor. He told me I still have cancer."

Sister Maddie gathered herself, and then she spoke with great pain in her voice, "Pastor, I want to know who lied, the speaker or God?"

A few months later, I officiated at Sister Maddie's funeral. Those last months could have been filled with faith and gratitude for God's kindness during her sickness, but instead, she felt devastated by disappointment.

In contrast, let me share a similar story with a different ending. A dear lady who was one of the "mothers of our church" (the designation for the faithful women who are the heart and soul of our church) had been battling cancer for a number of years, and her condition gradually deteriorated. I was in the room with Mother George and her grandchildren when the doctor examined her and made the sad announcement that it was time to call hospice because the end was near. I don't know how many people in the church had been praying for her recovery, but it was a lot. At that moment, I prayed again, and her grandkids joined me in asking God for a miracle. When we finished, she was smiling. Her voice was soft and weak, so I leaned over to hear her. The grandchildren didn't want to miss anything, so they drew close, too. She whispered, "Y'all keep praying that way. That's just fine, but I believe God is going to heal me in a different way." I could see a bit of a twinkle in her eye. She turned to her grandkids and explained, "Going to heaven is the ultimate healing. That's where

I'm going, so your prayers will be answered." She paused for a few seconds and then asked them one of the most profound questions I've ever heard: "Would you be okay with God if he takes me home?" She wasn't heartbroken. She wasn't devastated. She wasn't angry. She was supremely confident in the presence and promises of God.

At that moment, I thought of Paul's bold comment in his letter to the Philippians: "For to me to live is Christ, and to die is gain. If I am to live in the flesh, that means fruitful labor for me. Yet which I shall choose I cannot tell. I am hard pressed between the two. My desire is to depart and be with Christ, for that is far better" (Philippians 1:21-23). To Paul—and to Mother George—life or death was a secondary concern. Knowing God is all that mattered.

PITSTOPS ON THE ROAD TO RESILIENCE

I wonder how a lot of churches would respond if people like Jacob and his mother Rebekah walked through the doors on a Sunday morning. The gossip would be flying! The young man had cheated his brother Esau out of his inheritance by playing a trick on his elderly father Isaac . . . and his mother was a co-conspirator! Unsurprisingly, the family blew up: Jacob had to run away, Isaac was horrified and heartbroken, Esau was so angry that he wanted to kill his little brother, and Rebekah must have been caught in the backwash of the men's fury. If there was ever anyone who wouldn't have looked like a good candidate for Sunday school, it was Jacob! He had caused tremendous pain . . . in his own life and in the lives of every person in his family.

But God hadn't given up on Jacob. In an astonishing series of events, God broke through to make himself known to the selfish, fearful man.

First stop: Seeing God

Jacob fled to live with his uncle Laban. He had stolen the blessing of his father's inheritance, but in a twist of fate, he was now homeless and destitute. On the way to Laban's home, he camped out and used a stone for a pillow. That night, God showed up. The writer tells us:

> And he dreamed, and behold, there was a ladder set up on the earth, and the top of it reached to heaven. And behold, the angels of God were ascending and descending on it! And behold, the Lord stood above it and said, "I am the Lord, the God of Abraham your father and the God of Isaac. The land on which you lie I will give to you and to your offspring. Your offspring shall be like the dust of the earth, and you shall spread abroad to the west and to the east and to the north and to the south, and in you and your offspring shall all the families of the earth be blessed. Behold, I am with you and will keep you wherever you go, and will bring you back to this land. For I will not leave you until I have done what I have promised you." (Genesis 28:12-15)

Jacob may have been a cheat, a liar, and a fool, but he wasn't blind. When he woke up, he was shocked that God had appeared to him: "Surely the Lord is in this place, and I did not know it. . . . How awesome is this place! This is none other than the house of God, and this is the gate of heaven" (vv. 16-17). He called the place Bethel, which means "house of God."

Second stop: Submitting to God

During years of working for his uncle, Jacob had married and had eleven sons. He shrewdly bred Laban's sheep to keep most of them for himself, and tension between them rose to the boiling point. Jacob decided to return home, but he had no idea if Esau would take the opportunity to finally finish him off. At one point on the journey, he learned that his brother was nearby. That night, he sent everyone across the river and stayed alone. The Bible tells us, "A man wrestled with him until the breaking of the day. When the man saw that he did not prevail against Jacob, he touched his hip socket, and Jacob's hip was put out of joint as he wrestled with him" (Genesis 32:24-25). In the dark, Jacob couldn't tell who had hurt him. He asked the man to give his name, but he got an answer he didn't expect. Jacob called the place Peniel, "For I have seen God face to face, and yet my life has been delivered" (v. 30).

From that day forward, two things were radically different in Jacob's life: his heart was transformed because he encountered God . . . and he would always limp as a reminder that God was greater—much greater—than himself. The transformation produced a willingness to relinquish control and submit to God. (Isn't that what our wrestling with God is always about?) The deceiver faced Truth, the conniver encountered Honor, and the trickster found Love. At the same time, God created a way to remind Jacob of this monumental change of heart. I know people who have suffered disintegration of a hip joint, and they report that it's extremely painful. Every step pounds the socket and shocks the nerves. Jacob felt that stabbing pain with every step for the rest of his life. Some assume that every health problem comes from the hand of Satan, but this one surely was from God's gracious hand and was designed to remind a scheming, lying, conniving person that knowing the God of infinite power and grace changes everything.

I can easily admit that the biggest problems in my life have come because I resisted turning control over to God—I trusted that I knew more than he did! In those moments, I had a choice: to continue to resist him or resolve to let him produce resilience in me. When I was a boy, I did a lot of really dumb things, and one of them was playing a game we called "Uncle." One guy would bend another guy's fingers back until he couldn't stand the pain, and he'd yell, "Uncle!" I believe that God infuses pain into our lives to the point that we'll say "Uncle!" and submit our hearts and our agendas to him. In that sense, all of us are playing Uncle: every day we wrestle with the monumental questions of who will be in control and what will it take for us to submit to God.

I'm amazed at God's kindness and patience at this moment in Jacob's life. He let Jacob wrestle with him all night, but in the end, God used the contest to show the previously self-reliant Jacob that he *could* depend on God, and, in fact, he *had to* depend on God. By then, the day was dawning, and it was a new beginning for Jacob. To seal the deal, God changed his name to Israel, which means "wrestles with God."

In the brief account about Jacob in Hebrews 11, the writer says that at the end of his life, Jacob was "bowing in worship over the head of his staff" (Hebrews 11:21). He wasn't just using his staff for balance because he was old and feeble. Many scholars believe this was the way he reminded himself that God had met him, God had disabled him, and God had given him a radically new purpose. To Jacob, the pain in his hip was a small price to pay for his encounter with the God of glory.

What staff are you leaning on? It may be the memory of a failure when God finally got your attention and changed the trajectory of your life, or it could be the healing of a deep emotional wound, and like a scar, the memory is a reminder of both the pain and the restoration. It may be a particular avenue of service that came to you only because suffering gave you wisdom and compassion to care for hurting people. (Remember Tozer's words: "It is doubtful whether God can bless a man [or woman] greatly until he has hurt him deeply.") The life God gives us is a paradox and a mystery: we gain life by losing it, we accrue power by sacrificial service, we develop perception and compassion by suffering, and our pain is often the source of our greatest impact for God's kingdom.

Third stop:
Seeking God

Later, Jacob returned to Bethel where God first appeared to him in a dream when he was running from home. This time, Jacob commanded everyone in his company to "put away the foreign gods . . . and purify yourselves" (Genesis 35:2). And this time, Jacob wasn't looking for protection; he was there to worship the God who had been so kind and faithful all those years. He told his family and servants, "Let us arise and go up to Bethel, so that I may make there an altar to the God who answers me in the day of my distress and has been with me wherever I have gone" (v. 3). How complete was the restoration of Jacob? God repeated the change of his name to Israel, and then he said that Jacob was the heir of the grand, sweeping promise he had made to his grandfather Abraham: "I am God Almighty: be fruitful and multiply. A nation and a company of nations shall come from you, and kings shall come from your own body. The land that I gave to Abraham and Isaac I will give to you, and I will give the land to your offspring after you" (vv. 11-12). In response to being included in God's grand plan—redeeming people from

> The life God gives us is a paradox and a mystery: we gain life by losing it, we accrue power by sacrificial service, we develop perception and compassion by suffering, and our pain is often the source of our greatest impact for God's kingdom.

every tribe, tongue, and nation on earth—Jacob worshiped: "Jacob set up a pillar in the place where [God] had spoken with him, a pillar of stone. He poured out a drink offering on it and poured oil on it" (v. 14).

These three encounters with God turned a self-absorbed, foolish person into a full-hearted, generous man of genuine faith. On the night they wrestled until dawn, Jacob's purpose and direction were radically altered.

A resilient life doesn't start with us—our choice, our goals, or our initiative. It starts with God breaking in on our reality. Jacob's first encounter at Bethel revealed the *person* of God, the wrestling for control showed the *position* of God's authority over him, and the third appearance of God affirmed his *plan* for Jacob's life. In these pitstops, Jacob *looked around* and realized his life was in danger if God didn't come through. God invited Jacob to *look above* and see that God is worthy of affection and obedience, and to *look ahead* to realize his plan for Jacob went far beyond him to a world-changing legacy. Our resilience requires all three: a realistic grasp of our hopelessness apart from God, a fresh encounter with the God of grace and glory, and a renewed sense of purpose that our lives count for something far bigger than ourselves.

Our encounters with God probably aren't as dramatic as Jacob's, but they're just as real, just as powerful, and just as life-changing. Have you experienced the wonder of God's presence, position, pardon, power, and purpose?

A second question is like it: Has God given you a wound that reminds you to be dependent on him? Are you ashamed of your limp, or is it a treasure to you?

RESOLVE

One of the most difficult tasks in our lives is figuring out how to trust God in times of difficulty. Some teachers and preachers want to be optimistic, they want to inspire hope, and they want to appear to have a direct line to God, but they over-promise. It's my role to give people genuine hope and point them to the presence of God. He isn't faithful only when he answers all our prayers and gives us pleasure and prosperity. As we've seen, God usually uses the fires of suffering to draw us close. In his excellent book, *Walking with God through Pain and Suffering*, Tim Keller writes, "Over the years, I came to realize that adversity did not merely lead people to believe in God's existence. It pulled those who already believed into a deeper experience of God's reality, love, and grace. One of the main ways we move from abstract knowledge about God to a personal encounter with him as a living reality is through the furnace of affliction."[8]

A primary source of resilience is the willingness to accept whatever God brings into our lives. It's not that pain, loss, and death are good, but we trust that God *will use them for good*. In the Lord's Prayer, Jesus taught us to pray, "Your kingdom come, your will be done, on earth as it is in heaven" (Matthew 6:10). In the first part of that sentence, we actively pursue his kingdom values of kindness, righteousness, compassion, and justice, and in the second part, we're called to accept everything that happens as a messenger from God to humble us, test us, and strengthen us. Having open hands is perhaps the most challenging part of walking with God. A dozen times a day, we have choices to deny our selfish desires and choose truth and kindness. In those moments, we experience an internal war: Who is our master? What is our highest value? Will we settle for something less than God and his kingdom?

When Jesus was in the Garden after his final meal with his disciples, he spent time alone in prayer. He asked Peter, James, and John to pray with him and for him, but they went to sleep. In the darkness of that night, Jesus looked into the abyss of the hell he was going to suffer the next day. He could already begin to feel the pain. It wasn't a figurative hell . . . it was the eternal condemnation that all of us deserve for our sins. He had predicted his death many times, but on that night, the full weight began to crush him. It's no wonder that he prayed, "Father, if you are willing, remove this cup from me. Nevertheless, not my will, but yours, be done." In response, an angel appeared and strengthened him for the upcoming ordeal. Luke tells us, "And being in agony he prayed more earnestly; and his sweat became like great drops of blood falling down to the ground" (Luke 22:42, 44). He woke his sleeping friends again just as Judas appeared with the crowd of soldiers and officials. Jesus couldn't rely on his "trusted inner circle" for support. He needed divine enablement in the form of an angelic emissary to strengthen him. For us, too, there are times (hopefully not many, but surely some) when the people we rely on don't come through for us, and the only source of comfort, direction, and strength is the Spirit of God.

Jesus often invited people, "Follow me." Where do we follow him? Only to heights of joy? Yes, there, but also to give our lives to the Father and for others, just as he did, which may very well expose us to suffering and sorrow.

Walter Ciszek knew something about disappointment. Ciszek felt led by God to be a minister in Russia, but the church sent him instead to Poland. When the Nazis invaded Poland in 1939 and the borders with Russia suddenly opened, Ciszek thought his prayers were answered. He slipped across the border, but he was soon captured and sent to a Soviet prison, accused of being a spy. He suffered for five years in solitary confinement, then for many more years in a harsh gulag. During that time, God worked deeply in Ciszek's heart. He was tempted to be resentful and wallow in self-pity, but God gave him patience and wisdom. In his book, *He Leadeth Me*, Ciszek reflected,

Each day to me should be more than an obstacle to be gotten over, a span of time to be endured, a sequence of hours to be survived. For me, each day came forth from the hand of God newly created and alive with opportunities to do his will. . . . We for our part can accept and offer back to God every prayer, work, and suffering of the day, no matter how insignificant or unspectacular they may seem to us. . . . Between God and the individual soul, however, there are no insignificant moments; this is the mystery of divine providence.[9]

In the horror of the gulag, Ciszek came to know God more intimately than ever before. He was resolved to stay close to God . . . no matter what.

"BUT WHAT ABOUT ME?"

Some of us read about Jacob's encounters with God and exclaim, "That's what I'm talking about! I want God to appear to me, too!" Or we hear about God appearing to Moses in the burning bush, and we stare at our shrubbery in hopes that God will show up. But there has been, as far as I know, only one burning bush in the annals of history from which God spoke.

The paradox of faith is that God invites us into a genuine relationship, but it is, to say the least, a disproportionate arrangement! He is infinite in love, power, wisdom, and every other attribute, and we are finite, flawed, and fumbling in our pursuit of him. Paul captured this enigma in a beautiful prayer in the middle of his letter to the Ephesians. He prayed "that Christ may dwell in your hearts through faith—that you, being rooted and grounded in love, may have strength to comprehend with all the saints what is the breadth and length and height and depth, and to know the love of Christ that surpasses knowledge, that you may be filled with all the fullness of God" (Ephesians 3:17-19).

As I've interacted with people over the years, I've made some observations about how they relate to God. The common themes are study of the Word of God, being open to the Spirit of God, and a willingness to obey the directives of God, but I've noticed four distinct ways they connect with him:

- Sensors: Some people seem to have a sixth sense in their relationship with God. It's like they're hearing a radio frequency that's beyond most of us. This may be the spiritual gift of discernment, or it could be just the way God has wired them.

- Feelers: Other people have a very affective connection with God. When they read the Bible, pray, sing, worship, and interact with people, their emotions are supercharged, and they feel joy, sadness, hope, fear, and the rest of the emotional spectrum.

- Thinkers: I know some people who carefully analyze every doctrine, proposal, and situation. They don't rush into decisions. Instead, they ask plenty of questions, and if the answers aren't satisfying, they ask even more. These people dive deep into biblical truth and explore the applications to their relationships and the broader culture.

- Doers: And some people show their commitment to God by being the first in line to serve the poor, visit the prisoners, and care for the sick and elderly. When they read the Bible, they see a God of action who invites us to participate in specific acts of kindness.

It's helpful to take a look at these categories, but we need to be careful to avoid pigeonholing ourselves and others. All of us can pick up on God's whispers, all of us can be moved emotionally, all of us need to study, consider, and think, and all of us are called to be the hands and feet of Jesus to care for the disadvantaged. Still, when we identify our particular style of relating to God, we'll realize the others are different, but not deficient. The body of Christ needs all of us. And because opposites attract, we're often married to someone who is quite different from us! (Which, I'm convinced, is a reflection of God's sense of humor.)

EXTRAORDINARY IN THE ORDINARY

If we expect a "holy zap" of God suddenly appearing to us, we'll probably be very disappointed. The Scriptures and the lives of some believers attest to unusual manifestations of God and genuinely supernatural leading, but for the vast majority of us for the vast majority of the time, we hear more whispers than shouts and we see more shadows than substance. Gradually, as we grow in our faith, we learn to see the hand of God in the ordinary ebb and flow of our lives.

Jesus told us, "I will never leave you nor forsake you" (Hebrews 13:5). In response to his gracious promise, we can tell him, "Lord, I belong to you." Years ago, a pastor recommended that we carry that insight into every circumstance we encounter. When God gives us wonderful encouragement, we can rejoice and say, "Lord, I belong to you, and I realize you are the one who gave me this gift. Thank you so much!"

When we are lonely, we can pour our hearts out to God and say, "Lord, I belong to you, and I know you are with me right now."

When we are filled with self-pity, envy, or jealousy because life doesn't seem fair, we can pray, "Lord, I belong to you, and you have the right to determine my circumstances."

And when we face difficulties and excruciating decisions, we can tell him, "Lord, I belong to you, and I know you will lead me and use this situation to make me more dependent on you, no matter how it turns out."

In other words, we can experience the presence, peace, pardon, and power of God in every conceivable situation.

The spiritual disciplines of prayer, Bible study, generosity, meditation, and service are tools to focus our hearts on God, and as we participate in them, we need to make sure we're pointed in the right direction.

Let me offer this recommendation. For the next week . . .

- When you begin your prayer, say, "Lord, I belong to you. Speak to me as I speak to you."

- When you read the Bible, say, "Lord, I belong to you. Open my eyes to behold the wonders of your Word."

- When you give, say, "Lord, I belong to you. Everything I have is yours. Thank you for the opportunity to share out of the abundance of your gifts to me."

- When you serve others, say, "Lord, I belong to you. Use me to touch a life, meet a need, and share your love."

In past generations when the pace of life was slower, people found it easy to be quiet and reflective . . . not so much today! We live at a frantic pace, with our devices always on and calling for our attention. We need to practice a modern spiritual discipline: intentional disengagement. Unplug, turn off, and walk away from your phone, laptop, or computer so you can be still to think, pray, and worship. Some of us may find that we're addicted to the adrenaline rush of expecting the next tweet or post, so disengagement will be more difficult . . . but even more necessary.

Don't assume that God has abandoned you when you face trials. He's still there, he still cares, and he still delights in you. Centuries ago, St. Basil's faith was called "ambidextrous" because "he welcomed pleasures with the righthand and afflictions with the left, convinced that both would serve God's design for him."[10]

> Don't assume that God has abandoned you when you face trials. He's still there, he still cares, and he still delights in you.

I'm afraid that too many of us have settled for the trappings of religion without genuine encounters with the God of creation. We go through the motions with sporadic emotions but little lasting change. God may break in when we're not expecting him, and he always invites us to come close. In his most famous sermon, Jesus gave his followers a gracious invitation coupled with a promise:

> "Ask, and it will be given to you; seek, and you will find; knock, and it will be opened to you. For everyone who asks receives, and the one who seeks finds, and to the one who knocks it will be opened. Or which one of you, if his son asks him for bread, will give him a stone? Or if he asks for a fish, will give him a serpent? If you then, who are evil, know how to give good gifts to your children, how much more will your Father who is in heaven give good things to those who ask him!" (Matthew 7:7-11)

Do you want to encounter God? You don't want it as much as he does.

THINK ABOUT IT:

1. What are the particular challenges of relating to an unseen God?

2. Describe the three encounters Jacob had with God. How did God invite him to look around, look above, and look ahead?

3. Does putting his hip out of socket seem harsh to you? Explain your answer.

4. Are you willing for God to get your attention in a similar way to remind you to be dependent on him? Why or why not?

5. Would you identify yourself as primarily a sensor, feeler, thinker, or doer? What's the profile of each person who is close to you? Why is it important to appreciate the differences?

6. What are some reasons it's important to have an "ambidextrous" faith? Who do you know who has that? What impact does that person have on others?

7. What's the connection between encountering God and developing a resilient life?

Affirmation:

Lord, I belong to you. Speak to me as I speak to you.

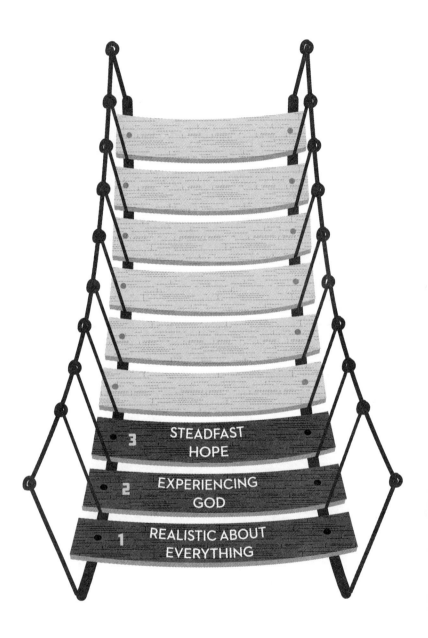

CHAPTER 3

STEADFAST IN HOPE

Truth offends everyone outside its definitions. But the
irony of truth is that the greater its potential for offense,
the greater its potential for giving hope.

—*David Jeremiah*

We experience all kinds of heartaches and setbacks that can crush our spirits. The third plank in the bridge to resilience is being *steadfast in hope*.

Resilience is created exclusively in an environment of resistance. I'm astounded at the resilience of Nelson Mandela. When he was growing up in South Africa, racial segregation and white domination were woven deep into the culture. Mandela entered the political fray in 1942 and joined the African National Congress two years later. His leadership skills enabled him to rise quickly, and in 1949, the ANC embraced his more radical strategy to bring equality to the country. He was arrested for treason, along with many others, in 1956. The trial lasted more than four years, and in the end, Mandela and twenty-seven others were acquitted.

When sixty-nine nonviolent protesters were killed by police in 1961, the ANC realized peaceful protests and a request for the constitution to be rewritten weren't reversing apartheid. In 1962, Mandela traveled to Britain to muster support for the struggle, and on the way back home, he received military training in Ethiopia. When he returned, he was arrested

on the charge of leaving the country without a permit and inciting work-
ers to strike. He was convicted, sentenced to five years in prison, and sent
to Robben Island. After his release, he was arrested again, this time with
ten others on the charge of sabotage. When he was allowed to speak to
the court, he famously told the judge: "I have fought against white domination, and I have fought against black domination. I have cherished the
ideal of a democratic and free society in which all persons live together in
harmony and with equal opportunities. It is an ideal which I hope to live
for and to achieve. But if needs be, it is an ideal for which I am prepared
to die."

The charge carried the possibility of execution, but when he and
seven others were convicted, they were sentenced to life imprisonment.
He was again sent to Robben Island, which had been a naval garrison, a
mental hospital, and a leper colony. Treatment of inmates was notoriously
cruel. The men worked in a limestone quarry where the dust and sweat
cemented their tear ducts. In an article written at the time of Mandela's
death, Bill Keller wrote that while Mandela was imprisoned there, "He
honed his skills as a leader, negotiator and proselytizer, and not only the
factions among the prisoners but also some of the white administrators
found his charm and iron will irresistible. He credited his prison experience with teaching him the tactics and strategy that would make him
president."[11] Even in prison, Mandela remained a political force in South
Africa. In 1985, he met with the Justice Minister and brokered talks
between the ANC and the apartheid government.

Three years later, still in prison, Mandela was diagnosed with tuber-
culosis. Finally, in 1990, he was released. Immediately, he rejoined the
struggle to end apartheid and minority rule in the country. He was
elected president of the ANC, and after decades of tenacious pursuit of
equality, the constitution was changed. He and President F. W. de Klerk
were jointly awarded the Nobel Peace Prize in 1993. The next year, he

voted for the first time in an election where he was on the ballot. He won and became South Africa's first president in an election encompassing all races and classes of people. In a remarkable demonstration of character and grace, Mandela invited one of his white prison wardens to his inauguration.

In a display of wisdom and generosity, Mandela joined Bishop Desmond Tutu to create The Truth and Reconciliation Commission to expose injustice and seek forgiveness for the cruelty perpetrated on both sides, but especially by the whites who dominated the nation for so many years. The panel offered amnesty for those who testified honestly about the crimes they committed during apartheid. The commission remains a model for all nations that have a history of inequality and racial oppression. Nelson Mandela never lost hope.

SPLATTER OR BOUNCE

Solomon wrote the proverb, "Hope deferred makes the heart sick, but a desire fulfilled is a tree of life" (Proverbs 13:12). What does it mean to have a sick heart? It can mean many different things, but none of them are good! People who have lost hope may be depressed, anxious, passive, violent, or suicidal. Typically, this isn't a passing, temporary condition; it's a pervasive conclusion that the future has nothing good to offer. People who have come to this place have lost their vision and passion for life. Hopelessness is a chronic spiritual sickness, and the symptoms affect every aspect of our lives.

Suffering and loss are common to all of us. From time to time—and for some, it's a lot of the time—we hit a wall, our dreams are dashed, and we wonder if there's anything to live for. I've heard it said that in those times, people either splatter or bounce. I've splattered before, and I can tell you, it's a lot better to learn to bounce!

Is there any real correlation between suffering and a refocused, renewed sense of hope? Yes, absolutely. In his letter to the Romans, Paul explains the gospel of grace so his readers, no matter their ethnic or religious background, will understand that salvation is God's gift. When we even begin to grasp the wonder of God's unmerited kindness displayed in the sacrifice of Christ, our hearts rejoice. We rejoice that our eternal destiny has been rerouted, we rejoice that we now have peace with God, and we rejoice that we have access to the throne of grace. That's enough, isn't it? Not quite. Paul then explains that God shows up in surprising places in surprising ways. He continues, "Not only that, but we rejoice in our sufferings, knowing that suffering produces endurance, and endurance produces character, and character produces hope, and hope does not put us to shame, because God's love has been poured into our hearts through the Holy Spirit who has been given to us" (Romans 5:3-5).

This is the ultimate bounce! When we stand back and see the God whose creative genius formed the incredible variety of plants, animals, mountains, seas and stars, we realize he's perfectly capable to reshape our worst times into something beautiful. We "rejoice in our sufferings," not because they're good or pleasant, but because they lead somewhere we want to go—they produce endurance (tenacity, steadfastness, resilience), which over time makes us stronger, wiser, and kinder, which again enables us to see God's hand in every circumstance. Seeing our situations from his perspective is the source of genuine hope, and it's not just textbook smarts. This kind of strong hope enables us to experience the love of God more fully and more deeply than ever before . . . and this is why we can rejoice in our suffering.

When I drop a rubber ball, the height of the bounce is determined by the force of the downward force—the greater the force, the higher the bounce. Today, many of us expect to bounce really high even though we don't expect to suffer any significant downs. People of great faith have suffered great losses, but they didn't give up on God in the middle of them. They learned to bounce.

THE LONG GAME

I believe there are so many encouragements in the Scriptures to "wait on the Lord" because it seems he is often agonizingly slow to act. Abraham's story is a case study in hope deferred. But that's not all—God's directions to him were frustratingly vague. Let's look at the story to see Abraham's amazing resilience.

Abraham (called Abram early in the story) lived in the Mesopotamian city of Ur. He married Sarah, but in a world where childbearing was the most important contribution of a wife to her husband, she was barren. God showed up with a startling directive: "Go from your country and your kindred and your father's house to the land that I will show you. And I will make of you a great nation, and I will bless you and make your name great, so that you will be a blessing. I will bless those who bless you, and him who dishonors you I will curse, and in you all the families of the earth shall be blessed" (Genesis 12:1-3).

God said "Go," but if Abraham asked, "Where?", God was saying, "I'll tell you later." God said, "I'll make you a great nation," but we can imagine Abraham asking, "Don't you know my wife can't have kids?" God was, in effect, saying, "I know. Just trust me." At that time, Abraham was seventy-five years old, and Sarah was sixty-five . . . already beyond the age of bearing children. But the old couple obeyed and started their trek west toward Canaan.

I'm sure they expected God to fulfill his promise immediately. After all, they were running out of time! But after years of waiting, theirs was a study in infertility. Abraham gave up. When God showed up again in a vision, he told Abraham, "Fear not, Abram, I am your shield; your reward shall be very great" (Genesis 15:1). God was saying, "Yes, I promised to produce a great nation starting with you and Sarah, but know this: I'm your greatest gift and your highest reward."

Abraham either wasn't listening or was so discouraged that he didn't believe God. He was done. It was over. There was no son, so there would be no great nation. He insisted on picking someone else to be his heir. In response, God reiterated the promise. He took Abraham outside and told him, "Look toward heaven, and number the stars, if you are able to number them. So shall your offspring be" (v. 5).

Abraham wasn't easily convinced. He asked, "How can I know?" In other words, "God, I've been faithful to you for a long time, and I haven't seen any progress in this nation-building thing. Help me out here!"

God's response is one of the most astounding events in the Bible. Let me set the stage. In the ancient world, agreements, called covenants, were blood oaths. In many cases, a king made a covenant with a vassal by having the vassal sacrifice an animal, which signified, "This should happen to me if I fail to live up to my side of the agreement." But that's not what happened when God initiated a covenant with Abraham. God told him to bring an array of animals, from a heifer to some birds, sacrifice them, and lay the pieces out in two rows. Abraham expected God to tell him to walk between the pieces, but instead, this is what happened:

> As the sun was going down, a deep sleep fell on Abram. And behold, dreadful and great darkness fell upon him. . . . When the sun had gone down and it was dark, behold, a smoking fire pot and a flaming torch passed between these pieces. On that day the Lord made a covenant with Abram, saying, "To your offspring I give this land, from the river of Egypt to the great river, the river Euphrates, the land of the Kenites, the Kenizzites, the Kadmonites, the Hittites, the Perizzites, the Rephaim, the Amorites, the Canaanites, the Girgashites and the Jebusites." (Genesis 15:12, 17-21)

God—the king—in the form of a smoking fire pot and a flaming torch, walked between the pieces. God was saying, "If I don't live up to my side of the agreement, let this happen to me. And Abraham, if you and your descendants don't live up to your side, this will happen to me, not you." I can imagine that Abraham was stunned. He didn't understand that God's promise was going to be fulfilled, first in his lifetime by God's faithfulness. Then, centuries later, Jesus, the Son of God, "walked through the pieces" and suffered the consequences of the unfaithfulness of Abraham's offspring—including all of humanity.

Let's not think that Abraham and Sarah were somehow different from us. They were just as flawed, just as doubtful. Twice Abraham offered Sarah to kings out of fear that they would kill him to take her. And at one point, Sarah was so disappointed in God's failure to give them a child that she told Abraham to have a surrogate child with her maid, Hagar, and he submitted to her demands instead of standing strong. Yes, they were just like us.

Twenty-four years after God gave Abraham the first promise of a child, three angels walked into his camp and reaffirmed God's commitment to come through for them. Eighty-nine-year-old Sarah was listening to the conversation, and she laughed when she heard them. But a year later, she gave birth to Isaac, a name that means "laughter."

When the apostle Paul wanted to illustrate faith in his letter to the Romans, he described Abraham's resilience to believe God even though the promise took twenty-five long years. He explained that God gave them a son when it was humanly impossible for the old couple to conceive:

He did not weaken in faith when he considered his own body, which was as good as dead (since he was about a hundred years old), or when he considered the barrenness of Sarah's womb. No unbelief made him waver concerning the promise of God, but he grew strong in his faith as he gave glory to God, fully convinced that God was able to do what he had promised. That is why his faith was "counted to him as righteousness." But the words "it was counted to him" were not written for his sake alone, but for ours also. (Romans 4:19-24)

When Paul wanted to show a picture of resilient hope, he pointed us to Abraham.

OUR LONGING FOR JUSTICE

Hope can be eroded by what seems to be unreasonable and unnecessary delays, and it can be shattered by painful experiences that make no sense to us. In those moments, we feel like the earth has fallen off its axis, and we're sure God isn't paying attention. We call it injustice.

God has put it in the heart of all people to be outraged at injustice. It's not a flaw, and it's not a sign of immaturity. It's good and right and normal. In fact, there would be something tragically wrong with us if we saw someone being abused and we didn't feel compassion for the victim and outrage at the perpetrator.

We see injustice all around us. We live in the wealthiest nation the world has ever known, but about fifty million Americans, including seventeen million children, don't have enough to eat.[12] A person suffers some form of abuse in America every nine seconds. One in four women have experienced physical violence by a spouse or partner. In eight of ten rapes, the victim knows the attacker. One in three girls and one in seven boys is sexually assaulted by the age of eighteen.[13] During the pandemic, about twenty million people lost their jobs, and many will never be restored. Almost half of those in the lower income strata have had trouble paying routine bills, while the lifestyles of those in the upper brackets haven't been affected much at all by Covid-19.[14] The Scriptures focus our attention again and again on groups that are regularly marginalized: widows, orphans, the poor, and resident aliens, and we could also add unwed mothers, the sick, children, runaways, the elderly, and other overlooked groups of people.

Many of us have a knee-jerk reaction to judicial authority because we wonder if the judge will be impartial, but in ancient Israel, people had the opposite reaction: they longed for the judge to come to their city to right wrongs and establish fairness. The psalms are especially rich in descriptions of God's love for justice. In an article for The Gospel Coalition, David Taylor writes:

> The fact that injustices occur every day will be obvious to anyone who follows the news. Injustices happen to individuals, mar institutions, and befall entire people groups. . . . For the psalmists, such a world is all too familiar, and they pray repeatedly for justice because they understand that a world full of broken humans and dark forces generates injustice everywhere and always. They also pray repeatedly for a just Judge to make things right. . . . For the psalmist, it is not simply that God cares abstractly about the idea of justice; it is that God *loves* justice and *does* justice. Psalm 37:28 declares: "For the LORD loves justice; he will not forsake his faithful ones." Psalm 99:4 proclaims: "The King in his might loves justice. You have established equity; you have executed justice and righteousness in Jacob."

Justice maintains the right of the weak, and it rescues the needy (Ps. 82). It rejects the desire to take advantage of the vulnerable (Ps. 94). The just refuse to speak out of two sides of their mouth (Ps. 28). They aren't bloodthirsty (Ps. 139), greedy (Ps. 10), or conniving (Ps. 94), and they don't love violence (Ps. 11). Those who love justice actively reject all systems that oppress people (Ps. 58).[15]

I believe most if not all of our hopelessness comes from our fear that justice will be denied. Seeking justice isn't optional; it's mandatory. The way we pursue justice, though, can be godly or ungodly, constructive or destructive. The prophet Micah lived in a time when God's people were in exile, and he called them to return to the Lord. He made it clear that just going through the motions of worship wasn't enough. God wanted to see a transformed heart which would then propel godly actions. Micah told them God wasn't pleased with lavish expressions of devotion that came from hardened hearts. Instead, he asked,

> He has told you, O man, what is good;
>> and what does the Lord require of you
> but to do justice, and to love kindness,
>> and to walk humbly with your God? (Micah 6:8)

To be steadfast in hope, God commissions us to do justice—not remain passive, not excuse perpetrators, and not close our eyes to the truth, but to take definitive action to stand against abuse and brutality and care for those in need. When we're involved in the lives of the marginalized with empathy, compassion, and generosity, we also love to see this quality in others. Giving our time and resources to prove we're good people isn't the heart God wants us to have for others. Instead, we should walk humbly with God, fully aware that we were aliens, far from God and without hope until Jesus stepped out of the glory of heaven to identify with us and do for us what we couldn't do for ourselves. The experience of grace reminds us where we've come from: we're no better than those who need our care.

GOD WILL BE JUST

When we see people being overlooked, marginalized, and abused, we wonder why no one does anything about it. We might assume that God doesn't care, that he's turned his head, or he's too busy to do anything about it. This conclusion shatters our sense of hope that a good and just God will make things right. Without this hope, we can become passive, we may medicate our pain, or we might try to do something about it ourselves—which is called "revenge."

> Without this hope, we can become passive, we may medicate our pain, or we might try to do something about it ourselves—which is called "revenge."

The first chapters of Paul's colossal letter to the Romans communicates the heart of the gospel, that Jesus stepped into our world to die the death we deserved to die and live the life we couldn't live. The closing chapters describe what a gospel-believing person looks like. Paul doesn't sugarcoat the reality that injustice is a very real problem—for the people in Rome in the first century under Nero, and for us today. But instead of giving up or lashing out, Paul offers a very different response:

> Bless those who persecute you; bless and do not curse them. Rejoice with those who rejoice, weep with those who weep. Live in harmony with one another. Do not be haughty, but associate with the lowly. Never be wise in your own sight. Repay no one

evil for evil, but give thought to do what is honorable in the sight of all. If possible, so far as it depends on you, live peaceably with all. Beloved, never avenge yourselves, but leave it to the wrath of God, for it is written, "Vengeance is mine, I will repay, says the Lord." To the contrary, "if your enemy is hungry, feed him; if he is thirsty, give him something to drink; for by so doing you will heap burning coals on his head." Do not be overcome by evil, but overcome evil with good. (Romans 12:14-21)

Angry people aren't thinking people. When someone puts out your eye, you want to put out both of theirs. In ancient times, the law of *talionis rex* limited retaliation to "an eye for an eye." This law was meant to stop the expanding cycle of revenge. But Jesus and Paul challenge us to get rid of revenge altogether and replace it with something far different: loving enemies, blessing persecutors, and praying for those who despise us. Paul doesn't tell us to say "Forget it" when someone hurts us. Instead, he says, "Take them off your hook and put them on God's hook. Put the person in God's hands and trust him to be just."

Can you and I trust God to be a righteous judge in a situation when we've been deeply hurt or betrayed? If not, then our instinct for payback will force us to take revenge . . . maybe not with physical violence, but through passive-aggressive means, like gossip. We feel happy and vindicated when we hear news that the person is suffering. The person must pay for what they've done, but the question is, do we feel compelled to be the judge, jury, and executioner, or can we trust God to handle it?

Some might argue that we should just "forgive and forget," but I'm afraid the human heart doesn't work that way. Similarly, the modern concept of tolerance doesn't help us at all. God has given us a deep sense of right and wrong, and we insist on people getting what they deserve. One of the most insightful concepts I've heard about the natural tendency to devolve into self-pity and the demand for revenge is from Miroslav Volf. He lived through the Balkan War where his younger brother was killed, so he had to wrestle with forgiveness and the urge for revenge. He says that the certainty of divine judgment is essential if we're to avoid the endless cycles of revenge. In *Exclusion and Embrace*, Volf writes:

> My thesis is that the practice of nonviolence requires a belief in divine vengeance. . . . My thesis will be unpopular with man in the West. . . . But imagine speaking to people (as I have) whose cities and villages have been first plundered, then burned, and leveled to the ground, whose daughters and sisters have been raped, whose fathers and brothers have had their throats slit. . . . Your point to them—we should not retaliate? Why not? I say— the only means of prohibiting violence by us is to insist that violence is only legitimate when it comes from God. . . . Violence thrives today, secretly nourished by the belief that God refuses to take the sword. . . . It takes the quiet of a suburb for the birth of the thesis that human nonviolence is a result of a God who refuses to judge. In a scorched land—soaked in the blood of the innocent, the idea will invariably die, like other pleasant captivities of the liberal mind . . . if God were NOT angry at injustice and deception and did NOT make a final end of violence, that God would not be worthy of our worship.[16]

The *emotion* of anger isn't wrong; the *actions* prompted by anger can be good and godly if they prompt us to speak the truth and pursue reconciliation, but far too often, our angry actions are designed for payback. When we're in this destructive cycle, anger soon turns into bitterness, which gives us two things we desperately want: identity and energy. We see ourselves as "the one who was wronged," so we feel completely validated in our self-pity, and the powerful emotions keep our adrenaline pumping, which gives us unusual energy. That's why bitter people can't sleep, their minds are often racing, and their lives are consumed by the hurt they've suffered and the hurt they want to inflict. What will stop this toxic pattern? Recently, I read a poignant statement: "When I was clever, I dreamed the desire of changing the world. When I was wiser, I resolved to change me."

THE FUEL OF CHANGE

Thankfully, God hasn't left us without resources to respond with wisdom, strength, truth, and kindness when we've been wronged. We can *love* people who act in unlovely ways to the extent that we've experienced God's love for us. John wrote, "In this is love, not that we have loved God but that he loved us and sent his Son to be the propitiation for our sins. Beloved, if God so loved us, we also ought to love one another" (1 John 4:10-11). We can choose to *forgive* only to the degree we're amazed that God has forgiven us. Paul made this connection: "Let all bitterness and wrath and anger and clamor and slander be put away from you, along with all malice. Be kind to one another, tenderhearted, forgiving one another, as God in Christ forgave you" (Ephesians 4:31-32). And we can *accept* those we might consider unacceptable only when we realize we were outcasts but Jesus welcomed us as his own. Paul explained, "May the God of endurance and encouragement grant you to live in such harmony with one another, in accord with Christ Jesus, that together you may with one voice glorify the God and Father of our Lord Jesus Christ. Therefore welcome one another as Christ has welcomed you, for the glory of God" (Romans 15:5-7).

Our ongoing experience of God's grace is the fuel of change. We're all on a sliding scale, and none of us perfectly grasps the wonder of the gospel, but we can all move a step or two along the scale as we realize we were unlovely because of our sin, unforgiven apart from Christ, and outside the family of God. We're more sinful than we ever wanted to admit, but in Christ we're more loved than we ever dared to hope.

Bitterness has poisoned countless marriages, ruined extended families, and caused

Our ongoing experience of God's grace is the fuel of change.

people in businesses and churches to be preoccupied with the wrong things. Injustice, in many cases, is an unescapable reality, but we can break the cycle by choosing to forgive. We began this chapter looking at the life of Nelson Mandela. In his memoir, he reflected on his commitment the day he was released from prison: "As I walked out the door toward the gate that would lead to my freedom, I knew if I didn't leave my bitterness and hatred behind, I'd still be in prison."[17]

It's human nature to believe we're superior to "those people" who hurt us. We'd like to think we'd never do anything like that to anyone! But superiority only makes us more susceptible to self-pity and bitterness. Jesus loved those who didn't understand him, who hated him, and who killed him. His heart broke for Pharisees and prostitutes, the overly religious and the irreligious. When God commissioned Ezekiel to go to people who had "a hard forehead and a stubborn heart" (Ezekiel 3:7), the prophet had a vision and felt an earthquake. This power, though, wasn't meant to blast the rebellious people. It was given to deepen Ezekiel's empathy. He wrote, "And I came to the exiles at Tel-abib, who were dwelling by the Chebar canal, and I sat where they were dwelling. And I sat there overwhelmed among them seven days" (v. 15). He sat in their seat and immersed himself in their pain. In many cases, we don't have empathy for hurting people because we're not willing to "sit where they were dwelling." We don't want to get our hands too dirty, we don't want them to demand too much from us, and we don't want to alter our schedules.

Our hope rests on the trustworthiness of God: his promises are *credible*, and he is *capable* of coming through when, where, and how he chooses. But God has given us "the dignity of causation"—he has given us a part to play in righting wrongs and caring for the underprivileged. Some problems can't be prayed away. Of course, prayer is important, but God has commissioned us to get involved, to reach out to care, and to be inconvenienced for the sake of people Jesus died for.

STEPS TOWARD HOPE

Restoring a sense of hope can be challenging. Whenever I speak on the topic of injustice, I can see the wheels turning in the minds of those who are listening. I'm sure the same thing is happening as you read this chapter—many of you are having flashbacks of the worst pain you've suffered . . . often at the hands of people you trusted. I'm not saying, "Just get over it." Not at all. As I've mentioned, the emotion of anger isn't sin. In fact, Paul commanded it! In his letter to the Ephesians, he wrote, "Be angry," but he realized this powerful emotion can quickly get out of hand, so he continued, "and do not sin; do not let the sun go down on your anger, and give no opportunity to the devil" (Ephesians 4:26-27).

The first step, then, is to acknowledge the event and the hurt, fear, anger, or shame it caused. Forgiveness is both a choice and a process. We may come to a point when we say, "Lord, I've been far too angry far too long. I trust you to be fair to this person, so I'm relinquishing my desire to inflict harm. I'm putting him on your hook." Author and pastor Lewis Smedes has written a number of excellent books on forgiveness. He says that any attempt to close our eyes (and our hearts) to the hurt may work in the short term, but this isn't genuine forgiveness. He explained, "When we forgive evil we do not excuse it, we do not tolerate it, we do not smother it. We look the evil full in the face, call it what it is, let its horror shock and stun and enrage us, and only then do we forgive it."[18]

And Smedes teaches that forgiveness frees us from a painful yesterday so we can envision a better tomorrow: "Forgiving does not erase the bitter past. A healed memory is not a deleted memory. Instead, forgiving what we cannot forget creates a new way to remember. We change the memory of our past into a hope for our future."[19]

In spite of the often quoted line, time actually *doesn't* heal all wounds. Grief does. It takes time and effort to grieve sufficiently and learn the lessons God wants to teach us. If the wound was deep or repetitive, we may need help from a Christian counselor—a professional who values the Word of God, trusts the Spirit of God, and supports the people of God. We'll learn that it's foolish to trust untrustworthy people; there are times when we need to challenge someone and times it's wise to just walk away—and it takes enormous wisdom to know the difference. (See Proverbs 26:4-5.)

What does all this have to do with developing resilience? Everything! People who are weighed down by bitterness and self-pity are very fragile. They don't splatter; they shatter! They may use their angry outbursts and demanding words to mask their insecurities, but underneath, they're deeply hurt and afraid. This description certainly applies to the victims, but it may also apply to a perpetrator who has been victimized years before. No one gets a pass, no matter how badly they've been wounded. We're all accountable to God for our words and actions.

We began by looking at the progression from suffering to hope in Paul's letter to the Romans. Now, as we look back, we see that the greatest lessons come from character-transforming experiences of heartaches. If we want to grow in wisdom, faith, hope, and love, we'll begin to embrace hard times as God's divine curriculum. We may not enjoy the classroom, but we'll be different people at each graduation.

I know what I'm asking you to do. You're thinking of your spouse, your parents, your children, your best friends, your siblings, and others who have shattered your trust through betrayal or eroded your trust by a thousand sarcastic digs, frowns, and critical comments.

For some of us, the circle of resentment includes someone we were sure would never let us down: God. But someone we love got cancer, was killed in an accident, or walked out on us. It's easy to blame God because, after all, he's God! He could have prevented the disaster, but he remained silent. He could have performed a miracle and made things right, but he didn't. Some people talk about "forgiving God," but I don't think that's the right concept. God is holy and good. He doesn't need to be forgiven, but he certainly can disappoint us. As we've seen, half the psalms are "wintry," filled with complaints that God hasn't come through like the writer hoped. Our task, then, is to pour out our hearts to God, to bring our worry and pain to him, and trust that he knows far more than we'll ever know. Grief is never quick or pretty, but it's essential whenever we suffer significant loss . . . including the loss of God not doing what we hoped he'd do.

Hope is like a beachball. Resentment, malice, self-pity, slander, and hatred are anchors that hold the ball under the water, but when the knots are untied, the ball rises swiftly and powerfully and bursts through the surface. It's not that resilient people don't have problems; it's that they've learned to trust God to transform their deficits into gains.

Injustice is a pervasive reality. In response, we can become more resentful or more resilient. The two are mutually exclusive. Are you untying the anchors so your hope can soar?

THINK ABOUT IT:

1. Describe a time when your hope was deferred and your heart was sick. And describe a time when a cherished hope was fulfilled.

2. Review the process Paul describes in Romans 5:3-5: "We rejoice in our sufferings, knowing that suffering produces endurance, and endurance produces character, and character produces hope, and hope does not put us to shame, because God's love has been poured into our hearts through the Holy Spirit who has been given to us." Rephrase the process in your own words, and explain how each stage is built on the previous one.

3. How do you think Abraham felt during the twenty-five years that God's promise of an heir wasn't fulfilled? How do you think his vision of the fire pot and burning torch gave him hope and resilience?

4. Does the teaching that God is a righteous judge help clarify your hope and give you more resilience? Explain your answer.

5. What does it mean to "put people on God's hook" instead of seeking revenge for those who have hurt you?

6. How would a deeper experience of God's love, forgiveness, and acceptance give you more resilience?

7. Why is it important to realize that grief is always a component of forgiveness? What happens when we try to quickly "forgive and forget"?

8. What's your next step in strengthening your resilient hope?

Affirmation:

God has put it in the heart of all people to be outraged at injustice. It's not a flaw, and it's not a sign of immaturity. It's good and right and normal.

CHAPTER 4

INTERVENTION FROM GOD

How can you live with the terrifying thought that the
hurricane has become human, that fire has become
flesh, that life itself became life and walked in our
midst? Christianity either means that, or it means
nothing. It is either the most devastating disclosure
of the deepest reality of the world, or it is a sham, a
nonsense, a bit of deceitful play-acting. Most of us,
unable to cope with saying either of those things,
condemn ourselves to live in the shallow world in
between. We may not be content there, but we don't
know how to escape.

—*N. T. Wright*

Are you ready to keep building your bridge to resilience? When we're
hurt, or angry, or ashamed, we may feel like God is against us . . . or that
he's a million miles away. He's not. He's with us, and he's for us. The fourth
plank in the bridge is an *intervention from God.*

Joni Eareckson was a happy, vibrant teenager who enjoyed tennis,
riding horses, hiking, and swimming. Her family lived in Baltimore, and
at a family outing at the beach in July of 1967, she dove into Chesapeake

Bay. The water, though, was too shallow. She takes us to the shore that day:

> The hot July sun was setting low in the west and gave the waters of Chesapeake Bay a warm red glow. The water was murky, and as my body broke the surface in a dive, its cold cleanness doused my skin.
>
> In a jumble of actions and feelings, many things happened simultaneously. I felt my head strike something hard and unyielding. At the same time, clumsily and crazily, my body sprawled out of control. I heard or felt a loud electric buzzing, an unexplainable inner sensation. It was something like an electrical shock, combined with a vibration—like a heavy metal spring being suddenly and sharply uncoiled, its "sprong" perhaps muffled by the water. Yet it wasn't really a sound or even a feeling—just a sensation. I felt no pain.
>
> [After a few minutes of confusion,] panic seized me. With all my willpower and strength, I tried to break free. Nothing happened. . . . *What's wrong? I hit my head. Am I unconscious? Trying to move is like trying to move in a dream. Impossible. But I'll drown! Will I wake up in time? Will someone see me? I can't be unconscious, or I wouldn't be aware of what's happening. No, I'm alive.*[20]

Joni fractured vertebrae in her neck and was paralyzed from her shoulders down. During two years of rehabilitation, she tried to cope with the harsh reality that she would be in a wheelchair the rest of her life, but she became so depressed that she considered taking her own life.

Friends came to visit her, and one of them shared a passage of Scripture familiar to many of us: "For I know the plans I have for you, declares the Lord, plans for welfare and not for evil, to give you a future and a hope" (Jeremiah 29:11). At first, Joni reacted in anger. She wondered how her condition could be consistent with God's "plans for welfare" in her life. But then she studied the passage in its context. She realized God was speaking to people who had been defeated in a military conquest and carried out of their homes into exile in Babylon. Some prophets tried to assure the people they would be free to return home very soon, but Jeremiah told them that was a lie. In fact, it would be seventy years before anyone returned, so they needed to settle in the faraway land, put down roots in their new circumstances, and bless the people who had carried them into exile.

Suddenly, the passage had far more meaning to Joni. She remembers, "I began to see that God's plans for a hopeful future for me weren't necessarily that I would be jumping up and down, kicking, doing aerobics, jumping, walking, or getting back the use of my arms and legs. No, God's plans for me go far deeper . . . a deeper healing, a precious healing of the soul. As I was pushed into the arms of God each morning . . . I wake up saying, 'Jesus, I can't do this thing called life. Please, help me. Please show up and give me your smile. Give me your strength because I can't make it through today.' Because I go to God with that earnest dependency every single day, no, every single moment, I experience the sweetest, most precious, most intimate union with Jesus Christ."

She views the Jeremiah promise with more clarity than she had before the accident. God will always prepare his plans for the welfare of our souls, even if our bodies suffer harm. She says that the moments of suffering are "splash-overs of hell," but "splash-overs of heaven" aren't the times of perfect peace and happiness. Instead, they are finding Jesus to be present, faithful, and kind when we encounter the "splash-overs of hell." She concludes, "To find Jesus in your hell is ecstasy beyond compare. And I wouldn't trade it for any amount of walking in this world."[21]

In her darkest moments, God intervened to change Joni's perspective, give her hope, and renew her resilience.

NEVER ALONE

Psychologists, psychiatrists, and life coaches all have very helpful techniques we can try to become more resilient, but Christians have far greater resources of the Word of God and the Spirit of God. Yes, we have agency, and we have responsibility to act, but the Holy Spirit is powerfully at work in us. Salvation is all of God—we bring nothing to the table, it's all about grace. But spiritual growth and building resilience takes both: our commitment and the Spirit's transforming power. Paul explained, "Therefore, my beloved, as you have always obeyed, so now, not only as in my presence but much more in my absence, work out your own salvation with fear and trembling, for it is God who works in you, both to will and to work for his good pleasure" (Philippians 2:12-13).

We don't *work for* our salvation; instead, we *work out* the salvation freely given to us by God. And we're assured that we're not alone. God gives us direction, encouragement, and strength to take steps forward. This short passage ends with the simple but profound comment that our progress gives God "good pleasure." In other words, each time we trust him and respond with even a modicum of faith, he smiles.

In the same letter, Paul reminds us that the greatest act of intervention in all of history happened when Jesus stepped out of the glory of heaven to take on human flesh and become one of us. Christmas isn't just about toys and turkey. We celebrate the astonishing fact the baby in the manger was Emmanuel, God with us.

In his book on the Gospel of Mark, pastor Tim Keller relates theologian William Vanstone's observation that we all desperately want true love, yet no one is capable of providing it. We aren't vulnerable enough, no matter how hard we try. However, Jesus was radically vulnerable and totally secure, so there's no manipulation in his love. Keller observes: "Nobody can give anyone else the kind or amount of love they're starved for. In the end, we're all alike, groping for true love and incapable of fully giving it. What we need is someone to love us who doesn't need us at all. Someone who loves us radically, unconditionally, vulnerably. . . . Who can give love with no need? Jesus."[22]

The incarnation of Jesus is the rock-solid proof that God has already intervened in the lives of men and women for all time, and it's perfectly reasonable to assume that he's still intervening in individual lives today. Are we looking for him? He stepped into a world where God's people felt like exiles in their own country because they were under the heel of Roman domination. They had splintered into fiercely opposing political and religious groups, and there was a yawning gap between the rich elite and the countless poor. Jesus didn't wait for things to get more comfortable before he came. He entered history at a time that has many parallels to our own, and he delights to show up in our lives today.

When God shows up, darkness is dispelled . . . perhaps more slowly than we'd like, but we realize the timing is up to him. As we look to him for love, forgiveness, wisdom, and power, he transforms us from the inside out: instead of fear, love; instead of anxiety, peace; instead of frantically running around, patience; instead of cruelty, kindness; instead of caring only about ourselves, goodness; instead of giving up, faithfulness; instead of being harsh, gentleness; and instead of impulsively fighting, fleeing, or freezing, self-control. And Paul says that there can't be a law restricting those positive traits because they're the product of the Spirit producing them in us. (See Galatians 5:16-24.)

> When God shows up, darkness is dispelled . . . perhaps more slowly than we'd like, but we realize the timing is up to him.

IF GOD HADN'T SHOWN UP . . .

Jeremiah's career as God's prophet began with a bang. The word of the Lord came to him, and God told him that he had been known and appointed to be his mouthpiece before he was even born. Jeremiah hesitated. He realized he wasn't qualified because he was so young, but God assured him:

> "Do not say, 'I am only a youth';
> for to all to whom I send you, you shall go,
> and whatever I command you, you shall speak.
> Do not be afraid of them,
> for I am with you to deliver you,
> declares the Lord." (Jeremiah 1:7-8)

Jeremiah began preaching about the need to repent about forty years before the Babylonians destroyed Jerusalem. There was still time to turn back to God, and there were some brief flashes of faith, such as King Josiah's return to true worship and banning idols in the nation. But when Josiah died, the people turned back to their counterfeit gods. Two mighty nations, Egypt and Babylon, wanted the gold in the temple, and Jerusalem was attacked by armies from a number of nations. Jeremiah wept over the unbelief of the Jewish leaders and the people, and Judah's kings fiercely opposed him.

Finally, after years of being mocked and scorned while pleading with people to turn back to God, Jeremiah hit a wall. He was so discouraged that he turned in his prophet's card. He accused God,

> O Lord, you have deceived me,
>   and I was deceived;
> you are stronger than I,
>   and you have prevailed.

I have become a laughingstock all the day;
>everyone mocks me.
For whenever I speak, I cry out,
>I shout, "Violence and destruction!"
For the word of the Lord has become for me
>a reproach and derision all day long. (Jeremiah 20:7-8)

Then, he metaphorically walked into the boss's office and quit . . . on the spot, without giving a two-week notice:

If I say, "I will not mention him,
>or speak any more in his name,"
there is in my heart as it were a burning fire
>shut up in my bones,
and I am weary with holding it in,
>and I cannot. (v. 9)

Jeremiah had come to a point where he was resolved to resign instead of being resolved to be resilient. But even then, he says that God's message was like "a burning fire shut up in my bones." Even if he wanted to escape God and his calling, he couldn't. It was still as strong as fire. But Jeremiah vacillated in his resolve. In his despair, he realized God would ultimately be just and punish those who resisted him:

But the Lord is with me as a dread warrior;
>therefore my persecutors will stumble;
>they will not overcome me.
They will be greatly shamed,
>for they will not succeed.
Their eternal dishonor
>will never be forgotten.

O Lord of hosts, who tests the righteous,
    who sees the heart and the mind,
let me see your vengeance upon them,
    for to you have I committed my cause. (vv. 11-12)

This realization caused the prophet to sing and praise God, "For he has delivered the life of the needy [that's me, God!] from the hand of evildoers" (v. 13). But his optimism in God's justice didn't last long. He then lashes out:

Cursed be the day
    on which I was born!
The day when my mother bore me,
    let it not be blessed! . . .

Why did I come out from the womb
    to see toil and sorrow,
    and spend my days in shame? (vv. 14, 18)

The prophet began with the *resolve* born of his calling, then suffered years of *resistance*, *resigned* his commission, briefly *rejoiced* in God's justice, and then *recycled* his despair. Jeremiah began with high hopes, but his expectations were dashed over and over again. That's why he was called "the weeping prophet."

You may be wondering, "Why is Pastor Craig using this discouraging passage to talk about the intervention of God?"

Great question. I'm glad you asked. God isn't present only when things are going well and we praise him for all the obvious blessings. God intervenes in the ugly and the grind. Jeremiah experienced the deep disappointment of preaching faithfully but seeing only opposition. The rulers didn't ignore him; they blasted him! This was ugly, cruel, and hard. And it went on year after year with only a brief span of encouragement. In the very next passage, God spoke again to Jeremiah to proclaim that his people missed their chance to avoid destruction by the Babylonians . . . and God didn't try to soften the blow. He commanded Jeremiah to tell them, "I myself will fight against you with outstretched hand and strong arm, in anger and in fury and in great wrath. And I will strike down the inhabitants of this city, both man and beast. They shall die of a great pestilence" (Jeremiah 21:5-6).

Now, it sounds like God has lost his sense of resilience! But he hadn't given up on his people. As Joni Eareckson noted, after Babylon destroyed Jerusalem and took many of the people into exile, some of their prophets tried to convince them that God would free them and they would return in only a short time. That wasn't God's plan at all. Jeremiah sent a letter that contained God's purposes and strategy for survival. Instead of over-promising, he told them to over-deliver as good citizens of Babylon:

> "Thus says the Lord of hosts, the God of Israel, to all the exiles whom I have sent into exile from Jerusalem to Babylon: Build houses and live in them; plant gardens and eat their produce. Take wives and have sons and daughters; take wives for your sons, and give your daughters in marriage, that they may bear sons and daughters; multiply there, and do not decrease. But seek the welfare of the city where I have sent you into exile, and pray to the Lord on its behalf, for in its welfare you will find your welfare." (Jeremiah 29:4-7)

This is the passage Joni studied and discovered the golden nugget of truth that God has great purposes for us even in our worst circumstances. God hadn't abandoned his people. In fact, if they obeyed and settled down in Babylon, they would bless the city with their faith and their faithfulness, and they would experience God's favor. In the tragedy of destruction and exile, God promised: "For I know the plans I have for you, declares the Lord, plans for welfare and not for evil, to give you a future and a hope" (v. 11).

Don't miss this: Jeremiah announced that he was quitting, but God didn't accept his resignation. In fact, he gave Jeremiah another mission, one that radically reoriented the people who were in exile. If Jeremiah wanted to measure success from the outside, his only real success was that the people in exile believed the message in his letter. But God was just as pleased with his tenacious resilience in speaking God's truth all those years when no one would listen.

How do we measure success? Pastors often feel good about themselves only if they stand up in front of large and ever-expanding crowds. All of us tend to value power, prestige, and popularity, but these only make us increasingly dissatisfied. God used Jeremiah to challenge the people then—and us today—about what's worth our affections:

> Thus says the Lord: "Let not the wise man boast in his wisdom, let not the mighty man boast in his might, let not the rich man boast in his riches, but let him who boasts boast in this, that he understands and knows me, that I am the Lord who practices steadfast love, justice, and righteousness in the earth. For in these things I delight, declares the Lord." (Jeremiah 9:23-24)

When his values become our values, and his actions become our actions, he's delighted. That's what matters.

All around us, even in our churches, people are obsessed with being the smartest, the strongest, or the richest in their circle of friends. In ancient times, a boast was the way people declared what was most important to them.

God says there's only one thing worth boasting about: understanding and knowing him. And who is he? He's the sovereign God of creation, who is full of love, justice, and righteousness. When his values become our values, and his actions become our actions, he's delighted. That's what matters.

DETERMINATION AND DISCIPLINE

We live in an "in between time" when we experience both agony and ecstasy, heartaches and hope. Theologians observe that this is the period of "the already and the not yet." God has, indeed, given us grand promises, but some of them won't be fulfilled in this lifetime. As we walk in this life, we have the presence of the Spirit of Christ, but it's only a down payment—someday we'll see him face to face. In this life, we have "peace that passes understanding," but someday all tears will be wiped away and death will be no more. In this life, we have a purpose to expand and deepen the kingdom of God, but someday we'll actually live with the King! Resilience fades when we expect too much in the already, and we're deeply disappointed that at least some promises won't be fulfilled until the not yet. God intervenes through his Word, his Spirit, and through the wise, mature people of God, but instead of taking pain away, he promises to use our pain redemptively to conform us a little more into the image of Christ. As we experience God's presence and purpose, we love a little more, we forgive more completely, and we care for people who aren't like us at all.

In the ugly and the grind, we're tempted to give up. Those moments are pivotal points in our walks with God and our impact on the people around us. I believe the spiritual disciplines keep us grounded. As we pray, read the Scriptures, give, serve, and spend time with other believers, we may not feel a surge of optimism, but gradually, like Jeremiah, we sense God's presence and purpose, and we serve as his hands, feet, and voice.

During the Covid-19 pandemic (which, to some extent, we will probably be living with for years to come), many people took supplements and vitamins, but in many cases, they built up their immunity while isolation diminished their sense of community. They may have become more physically resilient, but the statistics about mental health during the crisis show that millions of us lost our emotional and psychological resilience.

If we're dedicated and disciplined enough to take a multivitamin every day to bolster our physical stamina and resist the virus, we can make the clear connection to our spiritual lives: we should be dedicated and disciplined enough to carve out time every day for prayer, reading the Bible, serving others, and talking to friends about what God is doing in us and through us as we build our spiritual resilience.

Teresa of Avila put things in perspective when she compared our present suffering to the unspeakable glory we'll enjoy when we're in the presence of Jesus: "In light of heaven, the worst suffering on earth will be seen to be no more serious than one night in an inconvenient hotel."

The Christian life isn't an engineering problem to solve. There are, to be sure, some very clear principles that guide us, but any study of biographies of people who have walked with God shows us that the Lord intervenes at his own pleasure and initiative. Jesus told us to knock at the door, and it would be opened, but we also see plenty of times when God shows up unannounced. We can build the fireplace, but God has to send the fire. It's up to us to be both passionate and patient, trusting, like Paul, that God will accomplish his purposes: "And I am sure of this, that he

> Jesus told us to knock at the door, and it would be opened, but we also see plenty of times when God shows up unannounced.

who began a good work in you will bring it to completion at the day of Jesus Christ" (Philippians 1:6).

As we've seen, disappointment is a reflection of unmet expectations. God is always present and always at work, but perhaps not in the way we imagined. When I'm disappointed, I ask myself: Were my expectations anchored in God's character or in my misguided hope of how God might work? Almost without fail, it's the latter.

We can find God in joyous births and sad deaths, promotions and layoffs, the kindness of strangers and the pain of broken friendships, in the ugly, the grind, and the glory. We don't demand that he fix everything now. What we want is only to know that he cares, he's for us, and he's working everything out for good in his creative, loving way.

THINK ABOUT IT:

1. Do you know anyone like Joni Eareckson Tada who has gone through terrible suffering but found God to be present and faithful through it all? What is that person's impact on others . . . including you?

2. What do you imagine Jeremiah was thinking and feeling when he announced to God that he was quitting?

3. We see him sometime later writing the letter to encourage the exiles to bless the city of their captors. What does this tell us about Jeremiah's resilience?

4. What are the truths about God that we need to recall when we experience "the ugly" and "the grind"?

5. What are some ways our pursuit of power, popularity, and prestige promise ultimate fulfillment, but actually suck the life out of our relationship with God?

6. What is the expected payoff of being obsessed with them?

7. What are the consequences in our most important relationships and our hearts?

8. Paul wrote the Corinthians that "light momentary affliction" is producing something magnificent in us. Do you really believe that? Why or why not?

Affirmation:

As we experience God's presence and purpose, we love a little more, we forgive more completely, and we care for people who aren't like us at all.

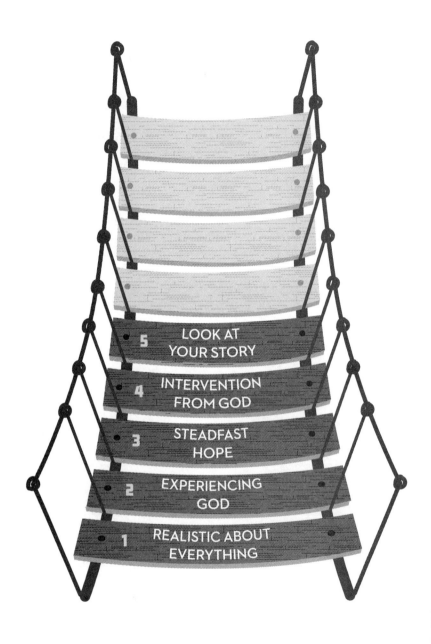

5 LOOK AT YOUR STORY

4 INTERVENTION FROM GOD

3 STEADFAST HOPE

2 EXPERIENCING GOD

1 REALISTIC ABOUT EVERYTHING

CHAPTER 5

LOOK AT YOUR STORY

**If you give it to God, he transforms your test into
a testimony, your mess into a message,
and your misery into a ministry.**

—Rick Warren

You may be surprised to know that your life—including your greatest
struggles—can become the source of tremendous resilience. The next
plank in the bridge of resilience is to *look at your story*.

From time to time, it's wise to stop to take an *introspective* look at
what's going on in your life, and take a *retrospective* look at how God has
led you to this point. In golf and tennis, the backswing determines the
quality of the shot. Coaches spend a lot of time helping athletes analyze
and improve this part of their game because it has such a powerful effect
on their performance. I was blessed to go to college on a tennis scholarship, and I remember my coaches working on my backswing from the day
I arrived until my last match as a senior.

We often think of qualities like hope, faith, and resilience as for-
ward-focused, but the level of our experience of these traits depends on
how well we've addressed the pains and disappointments of the past, the
proverbial "backswing of life." This is a challenging concept to many people. They've tried for years to forget what happened to them so they could

"just move on," and well-meaning leaders have told them, "Let it go." The problem is that the pain of the past isn't like a stick we can discard; it's more like peanut butter we can't shake off, no matter how hard we try.

I'm well aware that some of those who are reading this page have endured almost unimaginable abuse and abandonment. The very idea of going back to those events feels like being traumatized all over again. The past is like a backpack we carry. For some of us, the weight of the backpack is relatively light, so unpacking it doesn't take too much effort. Many of us, however, are carrying considerably more weight. We're lugging some pretty heavy rocks in there. And for some, the backpack contains a ten-ton boulder. We simply can't get rid of it without help, and even then, it takes time to break off parts of it and lay them aside. Sooner or later, though, even the heaviest backpack can be unloaded so the person can be free to engage in a fabulous future.

My wife's father was a cocaine addict for almost two decades. One of the most remarkable stories in Cleo's family is that her dad eventually became clean and sober. For years, he kept a picture of himself in his wallet, a picture taken when he was in the throes of his addiction. In fact, he took the picture the day he went to rehab. He often pulled it out to show people and told them he had been "a walking dead man." He wanted a constant reminder of the depth of the hole he had dug and how vulnerable he was even as a recovered addict. The picture was a visible demonstration of the starting point for his journey from despair to hope, bondage to freedom, the horrible parts of his life's story to the loud and clear message of God's redemption . . . even for someone like him.

In all families, the story of the parents is also the story of the children. When Cleo was a child, her father was a loving, attentive, responsible dad. She remembers, "In those years, he was a wonderful dad, so full of fun. On family vacations, he went to great lengths to make them special for all of us. Those were the best of times." However, when she was in high school and college, he was using. Cleo's family lived in Eunice, Louisiana, a small, rural community where everybody knew everybody. For years, the family was able to hide her father's addiction from people in the town. Her grandfather had built quite a legacy: he was a prominent pastor, owned a funeral home, and had about twenty-five properties. Cleo's father was an only child, so when her grandfather died, her dad inherited all of the assets. For families of alcoholics and addicts, the next line is a familiar one: her father lost everything because of his addiction.

When Cleo was in high school, she played on the basketball team. Her father attended every game and coached her from the stands. Even though he was using, he looked like all the rest of the fathers cheering their daughters. But when they got home, arguments between her parents filled the air, and she felt the powerful but conflicting emotions of love and anger, hope and disgust, compassion and shame. She remembers, "I wanted my dad to come to my games, but when I saw him there, I was afraid he'd snap like he did at home." Cleo remembers finding her father's stash of crack and pipes hidden in the house. She was equally hurt and furious as she flushed the drugs down the commode. When he couldn't find them and she told him what she had done, he wanted to reach into the commode to fish out the cocaine. At one point, the family had a blow-out argument in the street . . . for all the neighbors to see. That was when Cleo realized her father wasn't going to change without professional help. She also understood that she needed to work on her own life and try to write a success story for herself.

Cleo and her mother realized they had been enabling her dad's addiction by trying to ignore it and making excuses for him. He often stayed up all night using and slept it off the next day. During those tumultuous years, Cleo lost respect for her father, and their relationship became strained. Her mother couldn't take the lies and irresponsible behavior, so she filed for a divorce. Cleo looks back, "I always prayed that God would shake him so hard that he would come to his senses. I wanted God to do whatever it might take, short of taking his life, for my dad to turn his life around. I prayed, 'Lord, shake him but don't take him!'"

In college and during her first job in the C.I.A., she began reading the Bible more eagerly. She prayed, "Lord, I need you to teach me to handle the hurt, and after that, I want you to take away the memory of the hurt." Of course, she had a lot of rocks in her backpack, but gradually, she was able to take them out, grieve, forgive, and experience God's healing touch. When her father entered treatment and began to show definite signs of growth, Cleo also began to experience peace, profound relief, and emotional healing. God had taken away her anger and she forgave her father, so she could genuinely love her father as he took steps out of his addiction. During that time, her relationship with God became more intimate and powerful. The courage to look reality in the eye was essential for Cleo to develop resilience.

"The rest of the story" is that Cleo's father's recovery from his addiction became a platform to help others who struggled with alcohol and drugs. There was no more hiding, no more lying. He was very open about his previous drug use, and God used him to touch the lives of many people. He passed away in February of 2017, and his funeral was an outpouring of gratitude for the impact he had on people. The most painful part of his story had been transformed into a ministry of grace, hope, and love. This, too, is a story of surprising resilience shaped by the hand of God.

FACING THE GIANT

Virtually everybody in our culture knows the story of David and Goliath. Even if we didn't learn it in Sunday school when we were children, we've heard comparisons of this triumph to modern stories of courage. For example, Malcolm Gladwell's book, *David and Goliath*, "is a book about what happens when ordinary people confront giants. By 'giants' I mean powerful opponents of all kinds—from armies and mighty warriors to disability, misfortune, and oppression." He begins with the biblical narrative, but he uses modern people to illustrate each chapter— men and women "who have faced an outsized challenge and been forced to respond. Should I play by the rules or follow my own instincts? Shall I persevere or give up? Should I strike back or forgive?"[23]

We usually focus on the moment when David ran out into the field and used a stone and a sling to kill the armored giant, but it's instructive to rewind the story and notice what led up to this scene. Like our stories, David's contains a mixture of heartaches and courage. In his family, he was the runt of the litter. His father Jesse didn't even think of him when the prophet Samuel came and asked to see all of his sons. A moment like that never occurs in isolation. For some reason, David's parents or his brothers didn't see

> Like our stories, David's contains a mixture of heartaches and courage.

the potential for greatness in him. His only value was as a hired hand, a shepherd who stayed with the flock day and night. We get a small glimpse of his relationship with his parents in a psalm where he wrote with a combination of sad reflection and gratitude: "For my father and my mother have forsaken me, but the Lord will take me in" (Psalm 27:10).

In the opening scenes in the climactic story about the giant, King Saul's army and the Philistines were on opposite sides of the Valley of Elah. In those days, rulers often tried to avoid major bloodshed by sending individual soldiers as "champions" into combat. The victor's side enslaved the army of the conquered champion, but at least they were still alive. The Philistines didn't send one of their regular men; they sent a man who was head and shoulders (maybe two heads and two shoulders) bigger than anyone in Saul's forces. Goliath was a fearsome sight:

> He had a helmet of bronze on his head, and he was armed with a coat of mail, and the weight of the coat was five thousand shekels of bronze. And he had bronze armor on his legs, and a javelin of bronze slung between his shoulders. The shaft of his spear was like a weaver's beam, and his spear's head weighed six hundred shekels of iron. And his shield-bearer went before him. He stood and shouted to the ranks of Israel, "Why have you come out to draw up for battle? Am I not a Philistine, and are you not servants of Saul? Choose a man for yourselves, and let him come down to me. If he is able to fight with me and kill me, then we will be your servants. But if I prevail against him and kill him, then you shall be our servants and serve us." And the Philistine said, "I defy the ranks of Israel this day. Give me a man, that we may fight together." When Saul and all Israel heard these words of the Philistine, they were dismayed and greatly afraid. (1 Samuel 17:5-11)

For forty days, Goliath walked into the valley and shouted curses at Saul and his men, and for forty days, no one went out to fight him. The king's forces included the eldest three of Jesse's sons. One of David's thankless tasks was to take his brothers some food. When he arrived on the scene and gave the food to his brothers, he heard Goliath's threats. David also overheard some men say that Saul would give riches, honor, and his daughter to the man who killed the giant. Obviously, this offer wasn't good enough to prompt anyone to fight Goliath . . . until David showed up.

David said that he would take up the challenge. At that moment, his brother Eliab let all of his contempt for his little brother fly. He tried to shame him in front of the other soldiers. But someone told Saul about David's commitment, and the king summoned him. Saul didn't have much more confidence in this shepherd boy than Eliab had, but David responded, "Your servant used to keep sheep for his father. And when there came a lion, or a bear, and took a lamb from the flock, I went after him and struck him and delivered it out of his mouth. And if he arose against me, I caught him by his beard and struck him and killed him. Your servant has struck down both lions and bears, and this uncircumcised Philistine shall be like one of them, for he has defied the armies of the living God" (vv. 34-36).

David's past was checkered with highs and lows, courage and rejection. He concluded his statement to Saul with confidence based on his experiences: "The Lord who delivered me from the paw of the lion and from the paw of the bear will deliver me from the hand of this Philistine" (v. 37).

Saul gave David his own armor, but it didn't fit. David took it off, picked up his staff, a sling, and five stones, and walked out into the valley. Can you imagine what Saul and his soldiers were thinking at that moment? I envision some of them grabbing paper and a pencil to write home, saying, "You won't believe what's happening! A kid with a few rocks has gone out to fight the giant. I won't be home anytime soon . . . or actually, ever. In a few minutes, I'll be a Philistine slave."

We're all familiar with what happens next. Goliath's contempt for David sounded very much like Eliab's. David shouted back, "You come to me with a sword and with a spear and with a javelin, but I come to you in the name of the Lord of hosts, the God of the armies of Israel, whom you have defied. This day the Lord will deliver you into my hand" (vv. 45-46). David's first stone flew straight and true, and Goliath fell dead. The shepherd boy didn't carry a sword, so he had to use Goliath's to cut off his head. Saul's army quickly overcame their shock, shouting and pursuing the Philistines for many miles.

As I mentioned, the main scene in this story is very familiar, but we need to look back at what gave David the character and the courage to face the giant. If parents and siblings today treated a child the way David had been treated, we might call Child Protective Services. David was despised and disregarded by everyone in his family. He could have given up on God, on life, and on himself, but God used the pain of his past to build his resilience. It was a trait that probably had to be discovered before it could be developed, but those lonely, dangerous days and nights with the sheep gave the young man enormous resolve. His fights with the lion and the bear prepared him to win perhaps the most famous combat in history.

In light of his past, it's not surprising that David's relationships were both powerfully positive and destructively negative. His "mighty men" fought by his side when Saul chased them around the country to kill them (2 Samuel 23:8-39). Their commitment and love for each other is one of the most powerful stories of human connections in the Scriptures. Another beautiful relationship is between David and Saul's son, Jonathan. He was the rightful heir to the throne, but he loved David so much that he delighted in having him take his place. But of course, there was a dark side to David's human connections. While his army went out to battle, he inexplicably stayed at home, where he saw the beautiful Bathsheba bathing on a rooftop. He sent for her and had sex with her. After she told him she was pregnant, David ordered her husband Uriah (one of David's mighty men and a close friend) home so he could have sex with her and later believe that the child was his. When Uriah refused to have a privilege the other soldiers wouldn't enjoy in their homes, David plotted to have him killed in battle (resulting in the collateral damage of other loyal soldiers' deaths). David, the king and protector of the people, had become an adulterer, conspirator, and murderer.

Sometime later, the prophet Nathan confronted David about his sin, and to his credit, he didn't deny it, and he didn't kill the messenger.

Psalm 51 is one of the most powerful expressions of repentance in all of literature. Still, Nathan told David that his sin would have consequences. God had said, "You have struck down Uriah the Hittite with the sword and have taken his wife to be your wife and have killed him with the sword of the Ammonites. Now therefore the sword shall never depart from your house" (2 Samuel 12:9-10).

It's no surprise that David had problems with his own children. He hadn't had a good model in his own father, and the sins were passed down from one generation to the next. Among other family trauma he experienced, his son Absalom led a rebellion and tried to kill him. (And I thought I had trouble with my teenage kids!)

David is known as Israel's greatest king, the person God used to bring together the separated tribes into a powerful, united nation. It's instructive to us that in the moment of his greatest danger and opportunity, he pointed back at the past to renew his courage. And when he was confronted with his most destructive sins, he found that God is both holy and forgiving. David's reflections on the past and his understanding in the present are examples for us to follow.

> It's instructive to us that in the moment of his greatest danger and opportunity, he pointed back at the past to renew his courage.

ON THE DANCE FLOOR

It's not a stretch to say that at the core of our fallen human natures is the passionate desire to escape pain and responsibility. When God confronted our first ancestors about eating the forbidden fruit in the Garden, Adam blamed Eve, and then he blamed God! When God turned his attention to Eve, she blamed the serpent. Both of them were saying, "Hey, it's not my fault!"

Most of us have become quite skilled at blame-shifting to avoid responsibility. It's a lot like dancing—we choreograph our moves to look like we're doing just fine, but we're always one false move away from falling flat! It hurts too much to be honest about our wounds and sins, so we excuse ourselves or others ("I couldn't help it." "She couldn't help it."); we minimize ("It wasn't all that bad. No harm, no foul."); or we deny ("I don't even know what you're talking about. It didn't bother me at all."). These are attempts to avoid even opening our backpacks to see what's there. We keep the strap tied tight so we don't have to feel the shame of our sin or the pain of the wounds inflicted on us. So, we keep lugging the backpack around. We're exhausted by the weight, and we're preoccupied with it even though we pretend it's not heavy, but our anger, fear, hurt, and shame continue to fester, clouding all of our relationships and distorting our thinking about what's most important. (Do you know anyone like that? Sure you do.)

Those who have been involved in Alcoholics Anonymous point to Steps 4 and 5 as the pivotal moment in a person's progress. Those who wade into these challenging steps often make remarkable progress toward sobriety and restoration; those who don't usually quit at that point. In Step 4, people make "a searching and fearless moral inventory" of their lives. They're asked by their sponsor to write a personal history that includes the good, the bad, and the ugly. Nothing is off limits; nothing is left out. They address their drinking and its patterns, of course, but also every aspect of life: family, finances, faith, friendships, and so on. This step often surfaces roadblocks of pride ("I don't really need to do this. I'm doing okay."), shame ("I'm so worthless, there's no use in even trying."), and fear ("I'm afraid to open the lockbox of my past. I have no idea what I'll find out about myself!").

Step 5 is the determined revelation of what we uncovered in Step 4. This time, we admit "to God, to ourselves, and to another human being the exact nature of our wrongs." It's one thing to have the thoughts about our sins and wounds rummage around in our minds, or to take it a step further and write them all down, but it's quite something else to verbalize our dark secrets to another person. After all, this has been exactly what we've dreaded our whole lives! Certainly, we need to find someone who is both trustworthy and wise, someone who is mature and isn't shocked by sometimes horrific realities in our stories. For believers, this shouldn't be difficult to understand. The New Testament contains numerous encouragements to connect with others on a deep, supportive level. These "one another" passages tell us to love one another, forgive one another, care for one another, and generally be more supportive of one another. James, Jesus' half-brother, wrote, "Therefore, confess your sins to one another and pray for one another, that you may be healed. The prayer of a righteous person has great power as it is working" (James 5:16).

We live with an enormous paradox: we desperately want to be fully known and loved. To be known but not loved is terrifying; to be loved but not known is superficial. But we're afraid to let people in close enough because we're not convinced they'll hold our hearts with tenderness. The healing that occurs when we're honest with a trustworthy person is powerful and beautiful. We may have been afraid that if we told someone the truth about us, they'd run away in horror, laugh at our foolishness, or use the Bible to bludgeon us. But when we take our versions of Steps 4 and 5 to someone who shows understanding and compassion, we experience a little bit of heaven. After all, that's the very nature of God—he knows the very worst about us, and he loves us still.

When David tried to hide his sin, his shame only grew worse, and it clouded every part of his life. He reflected:

For when I kept silent, my bones wasted away
through my groaning all day long.

For day and night your hand was heavy upon me;
>   my strength was dried up as by the heat of summer.
I acknowledged my sin to you,
>   and I did not cover my iniquity;
I said, "I will confess my transgressions to the Lord,"
>   and you forgave the iniquity of my sin. (Psalm 32:3-5)

Isn't that what you and I long for?

TELESCOPE AND MICROSCOPE

When we look at our life's stories, we need to use a telescope to see the big picture—the full sweep of events and the impact of those events. And at certain points, we need a microscope to explore the details so we have a better grasp on what actually happened. Resilience is established by focusing on the truth, not excuses, lies, or ghosts from the past. Honesty is essential, but as I've mentioned, the journey for some of us will be slower than others, and we'll need more help along the way.

> Resilience is established by focusing on the truth, not excuses, lies, or ghosts from the past.

In an article in the *Harvard Business Review*, author and leadership consultant Ron Carucci describes the findings of his study of resilience in leaders. He found that people in stressful situations, such as leading an organization or facing the challenges of a pandemic, need this quality all day every day. He writes:

When we think about "resilience," we typically imagine bouncing back from major hardship. Management theorists have increasingly put forward a more nuanced definition, however: resilience as the ability to adapt to complex change. But in today's world, that means the demand for resilience is almost constant. With the ongoing onslaught of problems leaders face, and change being the only constant in organizational life, leaders must cultivate resilience as an ongoing skill, not just for the "big moments" of painful setbacks or major change.[24]

Those who are resilient, Carucci found, have studied their own stories, and they know themselves very well, including their character strengths, skills, the events or people who trigger disproportionate reactions, and their underlying convictions. People who don't have an accurate self-analysis keep reacting the same way to the same triggers over and over again. Uncovering the patterns of our thoughts, emotions, convictions, and behavior help us see that we have options . . . options that lead to better outcomes in our families, our work, and in every aspect of our lives.

Let me suggest a very helpful exercise. On a blank piece of paper, draw a line, and mark it off in ten-year increments. Find a time when you're not rushed or distracted, and ask God to remind you of particular events, both delightful and devastating, that happened to you during each segment of time. For instance, a friend's entries included fun family vacations when he was young, the time his father's business went bankrupt and his dad became depressed and distant, awards in high school, feeling out of place in college, strained romances, promotions, a beautiful wedding, his wife's PMS after their second child, his own depression, and God's gracious hand to restore him. Those are only a few of about forty events that came to mind as he thought about his life. Some of them came to mind very quickly, but others came only after being quiet for a while. Surprisingly, some of the memories seemed unimportant to him at first, but as he thought more about them, he saw the significance. He didn't rate them or sift them as they came to mind. He just wrote them all down and then reflected on each one.

That's the telescope. When you're finished, pull out the microscope and look more closely at some of the events. (You'll know which ones need some attention!) For example, my friend focused in on when he was ten years old and his father lost his business. He recalled that the temperature in the house rose to the boiling point as his father blamed himself for making some bad decisions, his mother was furious with him because the bankruptcy embarrassed her, and his brother began acting out in drinking and vandalism. As a child, my friend felt trapped in the whirlwind of all of those powerful emotions. He had nowhere to run, nowhere to hide. He felt it was his duty to lift his father's spirits, calm his mother's anger, and make his brother more responsible, but it was pressure no ten-year-old boy could handle. For years, he was driven to make top grades and excel in every endeavor to prove he was worthy of his parents' love, but it was never enough. He explained, "This analysis connected a lot of dots for me. I saw that this horrible season of my life had a negative impact on my identity, my goals, and my confidence. I'd lived with all of this for decades . . . until I took time to have a closer look. But that was just the first step. I also had to process the sense of loss I felt then and continued to feel even as an adult. I didn't feel free to talk about my feelings when all of that was going on, so as an adult, I had to talk about it, grieve it, and learn the lessons God still wanted me to learn from my childhood experience."

What do we love about our favorite movies? I think it's universally true that we love plot twists, the scenes when the courage of the protagonist turns tragedy into triumph. All of us are still writing our stories, and there are plot twists in each one. The shock of surprises gives us new insight into the narrative up to that point—we see more clearly and we understand more fully. In an article about "the science of the plot twist," professor Vera Tobin asserts that our "initial starting point for our reasoning—however arbitrary or irrelevant—'anchors' our analysis. . . . A major part of the pleasure of plot twists, too, comes not from the shock of surprise, but from looking back at the early bits of the narrative in light of the twist. The most satisfying surprises get their power from giving us a fresh, better way of making sense of the material that came before. . . . Remember that once we know the answer to a puzzle, its clues can seem more transparent than they really were. When we revisit early parts of the story in light of that knowledge, well-constructed clues take on new, satisfying significance."[25]

That's exactly what looking at our stories can do for us. We may be surprised, but even if not, we'll understand more fully how past events have shaped our lives . . . and then we'll have options to remain stuck or move ahead. The Danish theologian, Søren Kierkegaard, observed, "Life can only be understood backwards; but it must be lived forwards." That means we make our best guesses about our current decisions. For richer, deeper understanding, we have to look at events in the rearview mirror.

> For richer, deeper understanding, we have to look at events in the rearview mirror.

I know very few people who wouldn't benefit from taking a broad view of their lives and a closer look at particular events. Almost all of us have unfinished business that limits our resilience, and we have unwritten chapters in front of us. Does this level of self-examination feel like too high a hill to climb? Let me encourage you to take one step at a time, and find a partner to join you on the journey. As we commit ourselves to God again and again, we might pray the Serenity Prayer, penned by the theologian and philosopher, Reinhold Niebuhr. Many people are familiar with the first few lines, but I want to include it in its entirety. You'll see why.

> God, grant me the serenity
> to accept the things I cannot change,
> the courage to change the things I can,
> and the wisdom to know the difference.
> Living one day at a time,
> enjoying one moment at a time;
> accepting hardship as a pathway to peace;
> taking, as Jesus did,
> this sinful world as it is,
> not as I would have it;
> trusting that You will make all things right
> if I surrender to Your will;
> so that I may be reasonably happy in this life
> and supremely happy with You forever in the next.
> Amen.

Sometimes, we don't need to look back far to see an answer to prayer that strengthens us for today. When our daughter Corrie was two years old, Cleo and I planned to have another child. She got pregnant, but she lost the baby at only eight weeks. A year or so later, little Corrie was supposed to be in a Christmas program, but at a rehearsal the leaders realized she had a high fever. They texted Cleo, and she rushed to pick her up. I was out of town, so I couldn't help. Cleo rushed Corrie to the emergency room at the hospital, where she registered a temperature of 102. Soon a nurse called Corrie's name and carried her to a bed. She was limp and lethargic. When Cleo walked into the room, she looked at the heart monitor—it showed a flatline . . . no heartbeat. Cleo suspected she might be pregnant, so she prayed, "Lord, if you have to take one of these babies, please don't take Corrie." She then realized the heart monitor wasn't hooked up. The doctor gave Corrie some medicine and promised her a popsicle when she felt better. Only a short time later, Corrie asked for her treat, and she walked out of the hospital like nothing had ever been wrong.

Not long after the ordeal at the hospital, Cleo went for an ultrasound and learned that she was, in fact, pregnant, but there was a problem with the baby. She lost that one, too. The doctor expected Cleo to suffer a period of postpartum depression, so I watched her like a hawk. After a few days of my being overly protective, she told me, "Craig, you don't have to stay with me every minute of the day. I'm fine. The doctor doesn't know what I prayed when Corrie was in the hospital. Her life is an answer to my prayer."

We tried in vitro fertilization, but that didn't work. After our hopes were dashed so many times, Cleo told me she was done. We were resigned to the idea that we wouldn't have any more children. We were surprised the next Christmas to find that Cleo was pregnant again, and this time, she went full term and delivered Charlee.

Through the heartaches of miscarriages and the failure of IVF, our hopes took a beating, but God gave us the resilience to trust him—to cling to him—when all hope seemed lost.

Cleo and I aren't alone in our challenge to trust God in the middle of heartaches. All of us are somewhere on the rope bridge of resilience, and we have to trust God as we take the next bold step. In those times, we need to look back at how God showed up and provided for us in past difficulties because those memories provide a springboard to trust him now and in the future. We're wise to take time to ask some penetrating questions, such as:

+ How did God give me the wisdom I needed?

+ How did he provide strength and hope?

+ What lessons did God teach me in those times, and how can I apply those lessons in the challenges I face today and the uncertainties of tomorrow?

Remember that the power to propel you forward is based on power of your backswing.

THINK ABOUT IT:

1. How is living with emotional wounds and haunting memories of past sins like carrying rocks in a backpack? Can you relate? Explain your answer.

2. How did David's past experience with fighting a lion and a bear prepare him for the fight with Goliath?

3. How do you think David's experiences of abandonment and condemnation in his family affected . . .

   . . . his drive to succeed?

   . . . the strength of some of his relationships?

   . . . his vulnerability to sexual sin?

   . . . his relationship with Absalom?

   . . . his thankfulness for God's grace?

4. How have you seen people (maybe when you looked in the mirror) try to avoid or mask their emotional pain by minimizing, excusing, or denying it? Did it work? Why or why not?

5. On a scale of 0 (not at all) to 10 (off the charts), how eager are you to make a "searching and fearless moral inventory" and speak your truth to a trustworthy person? Explain your answer.

6. Take some time to do the timeline exercise described near the end of the chapter. After you complete it, describe what you learned about yourself.

Affirmation:

Resilience is established by focusing on the truth, not excuses, lies, or ghosts from the past.

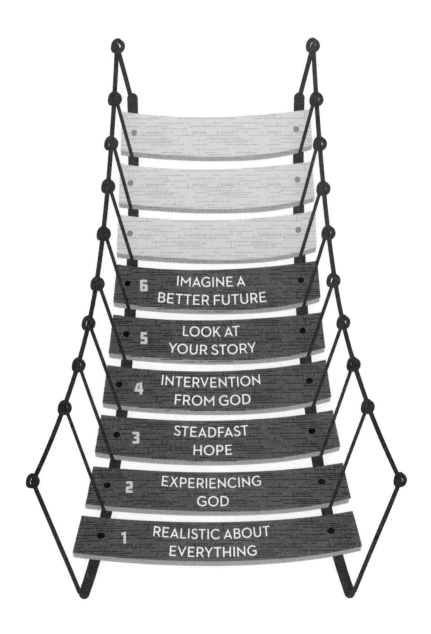

CHAPTER 6

IMAGINE A BETTER FUTURE

It was becoming clearer and clearer that if I wanted to
come to the end of my life and not say, "I've wasted it!"
then I would need to press all the way in, and all the
way up, to the ultimate purpose of God and join him in
it. If my life was to have a single, all-satisfying, unifying
passion, it would have to be God's passion.

—*John Piper*

When we lay the plank to *imagine a better future*, we pick up the pace and make more progress toward resilience.

In the last chapter, we looked back at our life's experiences to see how "ambidextrous faith" enables us to welcome pleasures with the right hand and afflictions with the left, convinced that both will advance God's purpose for us. We discover that the most important lessons we've ever learned were forged in the furnace of heartache, and those lessons enable us to see our future with renewed hope, increased patience, and greater effectiveness. In other words, we'll combine resilience with wisdom. In fact, a seminary professor observed that the greatest struggles we endure in the first half of our lives become the platform for our greatest impact on others for the rest of our lives. With this insight, we stop despising our stories of loss, suffering, and rejection. Instead, we see them as the different colors of paint on God's paintbrush as he artistically displays the significance of every event we've experienced. No matter how bleak and hard life has been—even if we feel we've lived in spiritual and relational exile—God wants us to imagine a better future because he is a God of hope.

THE POISONOUS FEEDBACK LOOP

All of us have internalized messages. Children are sponges who soak up the words and the nonverbal cues in their homes. Some parents have provided a wonderfully positive environment, and their children grow up with the firm conviction they're loved, they're competent, they're responsible, and their parents are proud of them. Some of us are on the other end of the spectrum: we've endured different forms of abuse or abandonment, and we've internalized very negative messages about who we are. Most of us are more of a mixed bag because our parents gave us conflicting messages. That's not unusual; they, like we, are imperfect as well as victims of the wounds inflicted by others.

To hide our pain and insecurity, we become experts at image management, wearing a mask so people can't see what we're thinking and feeling under the surface. But at the slightest provocation, our minds shift tracks and broadcast messages like these to our hearts:

"I can't do anything right."

"I can't afford to be wrong . . . or even to appear that I'm wrong . . . or I'll look foolish."

"I can't ever be vulnerable again. It hurts too much."

"I'm not as smart as . . . ; not as pretty or handsome as . . . ; not as talented as . . ."

"I only feel good about myself if I'm indispensable to someone who needs me."

"I can't afford to fail, or else."

"I'm helpless and worthless . . . a colossal screw-up."

"I have to win at all costs."

DO ANY OF THESE SOUND FAMILIAR?

These toxic messages create a feedback loop. We believe them, so we feel more driven or helpless, which makes us more susceptible to believe the messages the next time, which causes us to be even more driven or helpless, and on and on. This kind of internal messaging (also known as "mental mapping") severely limits our hopes for the future because we believe we're stuck in our failures and shame.

+ The powerful messages drive some of us to rampant perfectionism, trying to do at least some things better than anyone else to prove we're worthy of acceptance, but this also makes us critical of those who don't measure up to our standards.

+ Believing we're hopeless victims makes us passive and disengaged.

+ Believing we have value only when we sacrifice to care for others makes us compulsive in our giving and serving, feeling that we can never say "no" to anyone.

+ And believing that we have to dominate others to keep from ever being hurt again makes us driven . . . and angry at anyone who stands in our way.

In all of these strategies, our relationships suffer because each one has strings attached—we control others and are controlled by them instead of loving with full hearts and no strings to pull to manipulate each other. And these strategies weaken our capacity to be resilient. Left unguarded, we become victims of our *stinkin' thinkin'*.

A leading psychologist, Martin Seligman, identifies three damaging and distorting ways that we explain setbacks and adversity to ourselves. (He talks in terms of optimism and pessimism rather than resilience; however, the effect is essentially the same.)

Permanence: People who are optimistic (and therefore have more resilience) see the effects of bad events as temporary rather than permanent. For instance, they might say "My boss didn't like the work I did on that project" rather than "My boss never likes my work."

Pervasiveness: Resilient people don't let setbacks or bad events affect other unrelated areas of their lives. For instance, they would say, "I'm not very good at this" rather than "I'm no good at anything."

Personalization: People who have resilience don't blame themselves when bad events occur. Instead, they can see when other people, or the circumstances, are the cause. For instance, they might say, "I didn't get the support I needed to finish that project successfully," rather than "I messed that project up because I can't do my job."[26]

People who have already concluded they'll never succeed, that everything is a disaster, and it's always their fault tend to engage in toxic internal dialogue when they're under stress. In the middle of a chaotic, traumatic, or confusing situation, their resentment and self-pity eat them alive, and all they can see is defeat and dead ends. They live without any sense of hope, and their disillusionment is reinforced again and again by the distorted messages of permanence, pervasiveness, and personalization.

But there's a way out . . . if they'll just take it.

A BETTER MESSAGE

When emotionally healthy people read about God's amazing love in the Bible, they think, *Great! I know what that feels like, and God loves me even more!* But many of us can hear a thirty-minute sermon on grace followed with a two-minute challenge to obedience propelled by that grace, and we walk out believing that the preacher only talked about "oughts" and "shoulds." We're full of guilt instead of grace because our minds were programmed to shut out messages of God's love and accept only messages that maximize our shame—it's a form of "confirmation bias."

To some degree, since we're fallen people living in a fallen world, all of us have an "inner critic" who delights to condemn us, but for some of us, the critic is wired to loudspeakers! The first step in internalizing a better message about a better future is to identify the critic. As long as we fail to detect the source of these messages, we're doomed to believe them.

Usually, however, the source isn't that hard to identify. Most of us have recurring messages that pop into our minds at the first sign of failure, rejection, or opposition . . . like the list of internal messages I've already listed in this chapter. When we have the insight to see them and identify them as toxic lies, we can then open our hearts to the truth. And what a glorious truth it is! The gospel message is that we were helpless and hopeless, destined for eternal separation from God and without any ability to change his mind. Some of us committed the sins of the younger brother in Jesus' famous parable about the prodigal, such as selfishness, addiction, and rebellion, but others have committed elder brother sins of self-righteousness, self-pity, and resentment. But Jesus became our substitute: he paid the price we deserved to pay and died the death we deserved to die. The message of the gospel isn't just about that moment when our eternal address changed—it's about experiencing the grace, love, and power of God all day every day. (We'll get to that in the next chapter.) Meanwhile, let me suggest just a couple of new messages we can internalize.

Peter's first letter was written to Christians who had run for their lives when the Jewish leaders began hunting down and persecuting believers. They were desperate for hope, for a positive message from God. This is what Peter wrote to them: "But you are a chosen race, a royal priesthood, a holy nation, a people for his own possession, that you may proclaim the excellencies of him who called you out of darkness into his marvelous light. Once you were not a people, but now you are God's people; once you had not received mercy, but now you have received mercy" (1 Peter 2:9-10).

Those of us who aren't from a Jewish heritage may not see the connection to another pivotal moment in the life of God's people. During the Exodus from Egypt to the Promised Land, right before God gave Moses the Ten Commandments, God told Moses to give the people this message: "'Now therefore, if you will indeed obey my voice and keep my covenant, you shall be my treasured possession among all peoples, for all the earth is mine; and you shall be to me a kingdom of priests and a holy nation.' These are the words that you shall speak to the people of Israel" (Exodus 19:5-6). Like the refugees from Egypt, we're outsiders who became insiders because of grace. Now we are royalty, with the additional role of representing God to people, and people to God, as his priests. But that's not all: in both passages, God is giving us an incredibly positive new identity! In fact, the word "possession" in Peter's letter is the word "treasure" in Exodus. You and I are God's treasures! How's that for positive, biblical self-talk?

> **You and I are God's treasures! How's that for positive, biblical self-talk?**

In Paul's letter to the Ephesians, he pulls no punches when he describes our condition apart from God's grace: we were dead in our sins, under the domination of Satan, full of rebellion, and well-deserved recipients of God's judgment. That's the black velvet background where the diamond of grace shines most brightly. Paul described the stark contrast:

> But God, being rich in mercy, because of the great love with which he loved us, even when we were dead in our trespasses, made us alive together with Christ—by grace you have been saved—and raised us up with him and seated us with him in the heavenly places in Christ Jesus, so that in the coming ages he might show the immeasurable riches of his grace in kindness toward us in Christ Jesus. For by grace you have been saved through faith. And this is not your own doing; it is the gift of God, not a result of works, so that no one may boast. (Ephesians 2:4-9)

"But God" . . . these are two of the most beautiful and powerful words in the Bible. God didn't leave us to our fate. Jesus came to save us.

To describe our new identity, Paul uses the term "in Christ" or "in him" many times in his letters. We're "in Christ" in his death, so his sacrifice applies to us and our sins are forgiven; we're "in Christ" in his life, so his righteousness is credited to us; we're "in Christ" in his resurrection, so his vibrant, powerful life is ours; and in this passage, Paul says that we're "in Christ" in his ascension to the throne at the right hand of God, so he has imparted a degree of spiritual authority to us.

How's this for a new internal message that inspires our hope, gives us renewed energy, and propels us to a better future: "Because I've received the grace of God in Christ, I'm deeply loved, completely forgiven, totally accepted, and full of purpose"? Believe it, it's true. Memorize this state-ment and these passages, write them on cards and put them in your pocket, and repeat them to yourself over and over again . . . until they become ingrained in your thoughts, your heart, your attitude, and your actions.

EVEN HIM

There are few stories that are more poignant than Peter's. He was in Jesus' inner circle with James and John, and they spent more intimate, personal time with Jesus than anyone else. One of the high points in the Gospels was the scene at Caesarea Philippi (a location named after the most famous Roman emperors and the father of the Greek general, Alexander—all symbols of the world's power). Jesus asked the disciples, "But who do you say that I am?" And Peter responded, "You are the Christ" (Mark 8:29). Jesus was—and is—the King of kings and the Lord of lords, infinitely greater than the most powerful human leaders.

As the Gospels wind their way to the climax, we find Jesus spending time with his followers on the night he was betrayed. I can imagine the solemn sadness in his voice as he told them, "You will all fall away, for it is written, 'I will strike the shepherd, and the sheep will be scattered.' But after I am raised up, I will go before you to Galilee."

Peter jumped in to insist, "Even though they all fall away, I will not." In other words, "Jesus, you can't count on them, but you can surely count on me!"

Jesus must have shaken his head when he told Peter, "Truly, I tell you, this very night, before the rooster crows twice, you will deny me three times."

Peter again insisted, "If I must die with you, I will not deny you" (Mark 14:27-31).

An hour or so later, after Jesus' plea to the Father to "let this cup pass" was denied in the Garden, Judas led the crowd and officials to arrest Jesus. Judas kissed him, and the guards grabbed him. At that moment, Peter saw his chance to make good on his promise: he drew a sword and cut off the ear of the high priest's servant! Jesus, with remarkable composure, told Peter to put the sword away and he replaced the man's ear. As they led him away, the disciples ran into the darkness.

John and Peter showed up where Jesus was being interrogated. As Peter waited, he stood by a fire. A servant girl—not a fierce soldier or a powerful official, but a person who was marginalized in that culture— recognized him: "You also were with the Nazarene, Jesus." But Peter told her, "I neither know nor understand what you mean." She told the others standing there that Peter was one of Jesus' followers, but he denied it. A few minutes later, more people realized, probably from his dialect, that he was a Galilean. This time, Peter cursed and insisted, "I do not know this man of whom you speak." When he heard the rooster crow, "he broke down and wept" (Mark 14:66-72). Peter was crushed by his betrayal and shame.

On Sunday morning when the women went to the tomb, they were startled by an angel. He explained that Jesus had risen from the dead, and he gave this instruction: "But go, tell his disciples and Peter that he is going before you to Galilee. There you will see him, just as he told you"

(Mark 16:7). Jesus had given the angel this instruction so Peter would know he was still included.

John picks up the story sometime later. I believe Peter was so disheartened that he believed his future as one of Jesus' ambassadors was over . . . done . . . finished. He needed something to do, so he went back to his previous profession, fishing, and this time, he took six of the guys with him. They fished all night, but they had nothing to show for it. As the first light of dawn was breaking, they saw someone on the shore. He asked if they'd caught anything, and they yelled, "No." He told them, "Cast the net on the right side of the boat, and you will find some." I wonder how I would have responded to this seemingly foolish instruction from a guy who may not know anything about fishing, but the men were willing to make an adjustment. When they threw their nets this time, they caught 153 large fish! But that wasn't the biggest catch of the day. John realized this was a miracle, just like the one when they met Jesus years before. He told Peter, "It is the Lord!" Peter, our impulsive friend, put on his garment and jumped into the water to swim to shore. The catch of the day was Jesus reeling Peter in.

It seems the men in the boat made about the same speed to the shore as Peter because they arrived at about the same time. On shore, it was obvious that Jesus hadn't had any trouble fishing—he had already caught some fish, cleaned them, built a fire, and was cooking. He invited them to bring some of their fish to add to the banquet. Jesus told them, "Come and have breakfast," and they sat with him to eat.

When they finished, Jesus asked Peter to take a walk with him. I wonder how Peter felt at that moment. Was he excited? Terrified? Confused? Jesus asked him, "Simon, son of John, do you love me more than these?" We don't know if he was referring to the other disciples or the fish, but it didn't matter. Jesus was doing something remarkable to Peter. Three times, Jesus asked Peter, "Do you love me?" and three times, Peter responded,

"Yes, I love you." The third time, the weight of the moment hit Peter like a speeding truck. He remembered his promise to be true to Jesus unto death . . . and his dismal failures. His heart was broken. After each of the three questions and answers, Jesus reaffirmed Peter's identity as a disciple and restored his calling to represent Jesus to anyone and everyone.

Ten days after Jesus ascended into heaven, Peter was with 120 believers on the day of Pentecost. The Holy Spirit descended on them, and Peter gave the keynote address to all the pilgrims who had traveled to Jerusalem for the feast. Luke tells us that about 3,000 people believed in Jesus that day. The person who considered himself disqualified only a short time before launched the fulfillment of the Great Commission.

Peter had been a *failure* who was *forgiven* and was given a *future*. If Jesus was willing and able to change the trajectory of Peter's life, he can change ours, too. Like a rubber ball, Peter bounced back and bounced high. It doesn't matter if you've committed a moral failure, you're a thief, a prostitute, an addict, a Mafia hitman, or a self-righteous Pharisee—you can

> Peter had been a *failure* who was *forgiven* and was given a *future.*

be *redeemed, restored,* and *redirected* to a glorious future. Peter's story of resilience isn't how he pulled himself up by his bootstraps; it's how Jesus stepped into his gloom to address his past, affirm his present, and redirect his future.

THE QUAGMIRE OF SHAME

In my interactions with people over the decades, I've discovered that shame is one of the most spiritually and relationally crippling diseases of the human heart. Some people use the terms guilt and shame interchangeably, but there's a distinct difference. Objective guilt is the realization that we've *done something* bad; shame is the soul-shattering conclusion that *we're* hopelessly bad. Guilt has a remedy: repentance and forgiveness. But shame puts us on a never-ending loop of self-pity and self-condemnation, and the only hope, it seems, is to feel bad enough long enough about ourselves, which only redoubles our sense of worthlessness.

In John's first letter, he wrote, "By this we shall know that we are of the truth and reassure our heart before him; for whenever our heart condemns us, God is greater than our heart, and he knows everything. Beloved, if our heart does not condemn us, we have confidence before God" (1 John 3:19-21). A person with a condemned heart has no confidence in God, has a distorted concept of God, has little communication with God, and lives to hide from God.

I know what that's like because I was Peter. As I explained in the first chapter, my marriage fell apart when I was a very young pastor. I believed my ministry was over . . . and perhaps even my life. The Scriptures say that when Peter heard the cock crow, he went out and wept bitterly, and I know exactly how that feels. I had let down my family, my church, and God. I desperately wanted comfort and encouragement, but some leading pastors drove the knife in deeper. They told me that I had abdicated my position as a Christian leader, and I needed to find something else to do with my life. Their words of condemnation felt more powerful and seemed more sure than God's Word. I typed my resignation letter and planned to give it to the chairman of our deacon board, but first, I had to figure out what I really believed about God's grace and his calling in my life. After a lot of reading, thinking, and praying, I came to the conclusion that I couldn't tell people that God could forgive them if I didn't believe he could forgive me.

Is there a limit to the power of the blood of Jesus? Was this the unpardonable sin? Could his blood wash me as white as snow? Eventually, my heart matched Paul's testimony: "But by the grace of God I am what I am, and his grace toward me was not in vain" (1 Corinthians 15:10). Because of God's amazing grace, I can be completely transparent, and my vulnerability always points me back to grace as my source of safety and security.

Of course, I still got plenty of hard questions in my church. In a deacon's meeting, a man asked, "Pastor, how do you expect us to listen to you now?"

I answered him, "I plan to stand in the pulpit and preach to you in the same way you'll sit in the pew and listen—by the grace of God. Before my divorce, there was no other means or measure by which I could preach, and that hasn't changed. God's gift is apart from my performance. I don't deserve it. My *salvation* is by grace, and my *service* is by grace. I can't earn it, but God has lavished his grace on me, on you, and on our church." This deacon must have pushed one of my buttons because the words kept flowing. "What would we do with Peter, who denied Jesus? Jesus didn't give up on him. What would we do with Paul, who agreed to the martyrdom of Stephen and then launched a personal campaign of cruelty against believers before Jesus transformed him on the road to Damascus? What would we do with Jesus' family who thought he was insane? His half-brother became the leader of the church in Jerusalem. Paul reminded the believers in Corinth, 'God chose what is low and despised in the world, even things that are not, to bring to nothing things that are, so that no human being might boast in the presence of God. And because of him you are in Christ Jesus, who became to us wisdom from God, righteousness and sanctification and redemption' (1 Corinthians 1:28-30). I don't stand here in my own wisdom, my own righteousness, my own sanctification, or my own redemption. I stand here because I've received these gifts from the hand of our gracious God." This was, in my estimation, the most powerful sermon I've ever preached. I needed to hear it, and I think the deacons did, too.

Shame shackles us to the past, focuses our attention on our failure, and blinds us to opportunities for the future. Psychologist and professor Brené Brown has written extensively on this subject. She observes, "If you put shame in a petri dish, it needs three ingredients to grow exponentially: secrecy, silence, and judgement. If you put the same amount of shame in the petri dish and douse it with empathy, it can't survive." She teaches that it takes a lot of courage to shine a light on the sources of our shame: "We desperately don't want to experience shame, and we're not willing to talk about it. Yet the only way to resolve shame is to talk about it. Maybe we're afraid of topics like love and shame. Most of us like safety, certainty, and clarity. Shame and love are grounded in vulnerability and tenderness."[27]

LAUNCHING PAD

Grace is our launching pad into a better future, and it accomplishes this by freeing us from the past.

Grace is our launching pad into a better future, and it accomplishes this by freeing us from the past. When we want to hide our sins, repentance is a great threat because it exposes us. When we trust in our goodness, repentance reveals our flaws and makes us feel weak and vulnerable. But if we want to experience the wealth of God's great love, repentance is a precious gift that connects us again to the heart of God. There are, then, two very different kinds of repentance, and Paul describes them in his second letter to the Corinthians.

Scholars tell us that Paul wrote a letter to the church that has been lost. In it, he reproved the Corinthians for some significant sin, and after he sent it, he worried that the people would reject him and his message. Now, he has received word that they responded with humility and faith, and he's thrilled! In reply, he affirms them by describing a contrast between "godly grief" and "worldly grief." He wrote, "For even if I made you grieve with my letter, I do not regret it—though I did regret it, for I see that that letter grieved you, though only for a while. As it is, I rejoice, not because you were grieved, but because you were grieved into repenting. For you felt a godly grief, so that you suffered no loss through us. For godly grief produces a repentance that leads to salvation without regret, whereas worldly grief produces death" (2 Corinthians 7:8-10).

Godly grief isn't just being sorry for getting caught, and it isn't just being sorry to experience consequences. This kind of sorrow realizes sin has done more than break God's law; it breaks God's heart—it makes him sad because it hurts someone he loves: us. This kind of repentance reminds us of God's immense love, his delight in us, and that he considers us his precious treasure. It restores as it frees; it empowers as it comforts.

But there's another kind of repentance. Worldly sorrow crushes instead of restores, pounds us with condemnation, and inflicts even more harm on our hearts. Instead of turning to God for forgiveness and comfort, this kind turns inward, uses harsh messages to punish, and leaves the person longing for it to be over.

Godly grief says, "I messed up. I need to call my dad."

Worldly grief says, I messed up. My dad is going to kill me!"

To paraphrase the Puritan pastor, Stephen Charnock, "Worldly grief focuses on God's judgment and wrath; godly grief focuses on his goodness. A person who repents out of shame cries out, 'I have exasperated a power that is as the roaring of a lion, a justice that is as the voice of thunder; I have provoked one that is the sovereign Lord of heaven and earth, whose voice can tear up the foundations of the world.' But a person whose repentance reconnects him to the grace of God says, 'I have incensed a goodness that is like the dropping of the dew; I have offended a God that has the deportment of a friend.'"[28] Do you see the difference? I'm sure you do.

Unfortunately, in many churches, talk about repentance has gone out of style. Pastors emphasize subjects that are more comfortable to the average listener, topics that entertain but don't challenge. But an accurate concept of repentance . . . and the regular practice of it . . . frees us from the past and points us to the future. When we become skilled and frequent in our repentance, our minds aren't clogged by "what ifs" and "if onlys," and our hearts aren't weighed down by regrets from the past. For us, repentance shouldn't be rare. It should be the way of life. In fact, the first of the ninety-five theses Martin Luther nailed to the church door in Wittenberg says, "When our Lord and Master Jesus Christ said, 'Repent' (Mt 4:17), he willed the entire life of believers to be one of repentance."[29]

"The entire life of believers"—this reminds me of an airline pilot who makes a thousand minor course corrections on a flight . . . instead of waiting until the plane is flying over a different country! Luther and God invite us to make far more midcourse corrections.

Paul understood that repentance unhooked him from his past and propelled him into a fruitful future. Near the end of his life, he wrote his protégé Timothy, "The saying is trustworthy and deserving of full acceptance, that Christ Jesus came into the world to save sinners, of whom I am the foremost" (1 Timothy 1:15). Outside of Christ, Paul was perhaps the most resilient person the world has ever known. He had a horrific past, suffered terrible persecution and torture, and carried the burden of dozens of church plants on his shoulders, but the experience of God's grace carried him through.

No matter who you are and no matter what you've done, grace is the pathway forward. You may be a failure like Peter, a rebel like the thief on the cross, a murderer like Paul, a rigid Pharisee like Nicodemus, or a sex worker like Rahab who needed rehab—grace is the door to walk through to find more meaning and fulfillment than you ever imagined. Don't miss it.

Now, at last, you're ready to craft your personal vision statement. A clear sense of where God wants you to go helps you align every part of your life, gives you clear direction, helps you avoid distractions, inspires you to action, and provides benchmarks of progress. It's not a contest of speed. Take your time, look back at the experiences God has given you, identify your strengths, let your imagination roam, and ask God to open doors of opportunity for you. Remember that no one's life is a straight line, and all great stories have surprises, villains, and heroes. A resilient life takes all of this into account and keeps moving forward to honor God in every season, and the most painful parts of your past are the platform for a renewed purpose.

It may seem strange, but I believe we can learn some rich lessons by close examination of a familiar nursery rhyme . . . I prefer to think of it as "the hermeneutics of the itsy bitsy spider." If you're older than three, you're familiar with the poem:

The itsy bitsy spider climbed up the waterspout.
Down came the rain
And washed the spider out.
Out came the sun
And dried up all the rain
And the itsy bitsy spider climbed up the spout again.

This is an analogy of a journey from ruin to redemption, from heartache to hope. The spider had a plan and a purpose: to climb the waterspout, but it suffered the calamity of a flood. No matter how high it had climbed, it was knocked down to the bottom, but eventually, the sun came out—it was a new day for the spider! It went back to the same spout, but perhaps with new determination . . . and a sharp ear to listen for any approaching storms. The spider was resilient. Even after a major setback, it took advantage of the sun coming out. Hope was more powerful than disappointment, and the spider started climbing again.

Either you *have been* that spider, you *are* that spider, or you *will be* that spider—sooner or later, all of us suffer major setbacks. Like the spider, we don't need a perfect response, but we need *enough* hope, *enough* courage, and *enough* resilience to start over again. That's what Peter, Paul, Rahab, and other heroes in the Bible did, and that's what we can do, too.

THINK ABOUT IT:

1. How do you imagine Peter felt and what was he thinking when he saw Jesus on the shore that morning? How about as he sat eating breakfast? And when Jesus asked him the three questions?

2. Three times, Jesus reaffirmed Peter's mission to lead the church, and only days later he was the speaker at Pentecost. What do you imagine happened in Peter's mind and heart during those few days?

3. "Shame shackles us to the past, focuses our attention on our failure, and blinds us to opportunities for the future." How have you seen this statement play out in the lives of people you know, maybe even your own?

4. How would you contrast the feelings, goals, and effects of godly grief and worldly grief?

5. Are you free from shame so you can pursue the future? Explain your answer.

6. Is it attractive or threatening that repentance should be a regular and vital part of your daily life so you can make lots of midcourse corrections?

7. You may have a clearly formed sense of God's calling, you may have some general sense, or you may not have one at all. Describe how you imagine God might use you, especially in light of the lessons you've learned from past failures and heartaches.

Affirmation:

Grace is our launching pad into a better future, and it accomplishes this by freeing us from the past.

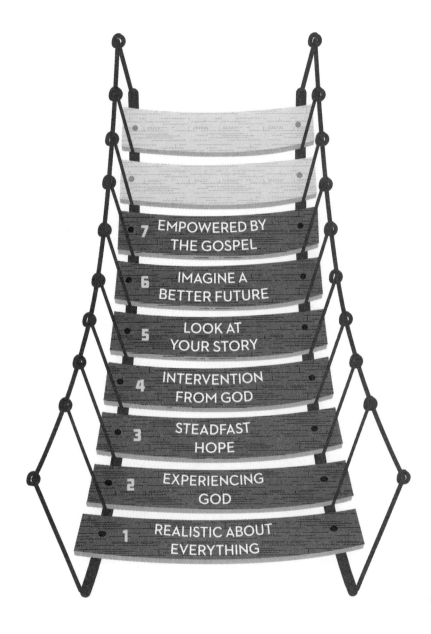

CHAPTER 7

EMPOWERED BY THE GOSPEL

God's unfailing love for us is an objective fact affirmed
over and over in the Scriptures. It is true whether we
believe it or not. Our doubts do not destroy God's love,
nor does our faith create it. It originates in the very
nature of God, who is love, and it flows to us through our
union with His beloved Son.

—Jerry Bridges

We aren't left on our own. God gives us the motivation, wisdom, and
strength to keep going when we're *empowered by the gospel*.

At a point early in my ministry, I realized the grace of God is much
more comprehensive than I'd been teaching. I certainly believed that we
are saved only by what Jesus did for us and we contribute nothing to
it, but it took me a while to realize that grace changes everything—yes,
everything.

Years ago, one of the main problems in the church was legalism, the
teaching that we have to obey a list of rules (and in some churches, a long
list) to be accepted by God. This led to some Christians becoming preoccupied with externals—movies, dancing, worship attire, tattoos, regular
church attendance, saying the right things and doing the right things—so

much that they missed God's heart. In recent years, fewer churches insist on such rules; instead, a type of moralism has taken its place. This is the assumption that if we're pretty good people, surely God will accept us. "Pretty good," of course, is on a sliding scale, and no one can really define it.

A few years ago, sociologist Christian Smith and coauthor Melinda Denton released a study that showed teenagers in America don't have traditional theological views. They ascribe to "moralistic therapeutic deism," a term that applies to their parents as well. *Moralism* refers to the belief that God primarily wants people to be good and nice to each other. *Therapeutic* means that religion's chief aim is to provide comfort and help, not forgiveness of sins and a God-focused purpose. And *deism* refers to the concept that God created the universe, but he's mostly hands-off now. As they interviewed 3,000 people for their study, they found five common beliefs:

- A God exists who created and ordered the world and watches over human life on earth.

- God wants people to be good, nice, and fair to each other, as taught in the Bible and by most world religions.

- The central goal of life is to be happy and to feel good about oneself.

- God does not need to be particularly involved in one's life except when God is needed to resolve a problem.

- Good people go to heaven when they die.[30]

This, I'm sure you can tell, isn't the message of the gospel! We need more than God winking at our sins and giving us a pass. We need unconditional love, forgiveness for every wrong, and welcome into the heart of God.

Years ago, a young lady who had sung in our young adult teen choir suddenly stopped attending our church. I wondered what happened to her. Over a year later, as I walked in the mall one day, I saw her in the distance. She was pushing a stroller. Our eyes briefly met, and I could tell she felt uncomfortable. I wanted to speak to her, but the look on her face told me that she wanted to turn and head in the opposite direction. But she didn't walk away. I went to her and we chatted a bit, and then I asked, "Whose baby is this?"

I should have known. She looked down and whispered, "Pastor, this is my baby."

I said something about how pretty the baby was, but she took the opportunity to explain herself. "That's why I stopped coming to church." She paused for a few seconds and then told me, "I was told that since I'm an unwed mother that I'm not welcome at church. They said I was a bad example to all the other teens."

I wanted to shake whoever gave her that condemning, excluding message. How can we tell people that abortion is wrong and then punish a young girl for keeping her baby? I asked her to sit with me in the middle of the mall atrium so I could tell her again about the love of God. I said, "There's nothing you can do to make God love you more than he already does. And there's nothing you can do to make him love you less."

She began weeping. Dozens of pairs of eyes turned to us, but neither of us was distracted from this holy moment. I continued, "And let me assure you, God loves your baby. Your baby isn't cursed, and she's not an object of God's displeasure. This child isn't a penalty or a problem. Your baby is God's delight." Her tears continued to flow.

As I mentioned earlier, in the African-American community, we have "mothers of the church," older ladies who are the matriarchs of the congregation. On the first Sunday of each month when we have communion, they're dressed up in their finest, with white hats and gloves, sitting on the front row. I reminded this young mother about these women. She nodded, and then I told her, "Have you ever noticed that some of those ladies have children with different last names? And did you know that some of the deacons who pass out the communion elements have children whose names aren't the same as theirs?" She looked at me with her eyes wide open. I then told her, "Let me tell you about all this. When they were younger, those ladies and those men had relationships with people they didn't eventually marry. Today, those mothers of the church and those deacons have put enough time between the sin of their youth and their present service to the church that no one even notices anymore. They made mistakes in the past, but God is using them to expand his kingdom. Let me assure you that God isn't finished with you. He loves you dearly, and he has a magnificent future for you."

The next Sunday morning, she came to church with her little baby. I had shared the gospel of grace with her—not only for salvation, but to navigate the turbulent waters of life—and she believed. I shared the gospel of grace, which gave her buoyancy and the ability to experience the restorative, redemptive, and resilient power of God's love. I had to be honest in sharing with her that sex before marriage is a sin against God—and it breaks the heart of God. However, God's unconditional and undeserving grace can pardon every sin, even that one. The "church service" we had in the atrium of the mall was every bit as profound as anything she could hear in our building on Sunday mornings.

To take things one more step for this young woman and her child, I dedicated her baby during a church service. For years, it had been church policy that we wouldn't dedicate the child of an unwed mother, but that was misguided and graceless. I was thrilled to tell this young mom and our congregation that God delights in her child and our church is committed to support her and her baby. This was a powerful message of love and inclusion to her, to the mothers of the church, the deacons, and everyone else in our body of believers.

THE G.O.A.T.

Jesus was and is the embodiment of the gospel of grace. He was the most resilient person the world has ever known . . . or will ever know. He turned the ideas of power, love, and honor upside down. Jesus was the King with ultimate authority, but he was born to peasants and his first crib was a feeding trough. He announced the arrival of a glorious kingdom, but it was one that would be realized through sacrifice and suffering. He wasn't surprised when even his closest followers didn't understand him or when his opponents plotted to kill him. He gave all for all. He is the Greatest of All Time.

Jesus' offer of grace is staggering—and if we're not staggered by it, we haven't yet grasped it. Sadly, many people in our churches have reduced the power of grace to only God's assistance in a self-improvement project. They believe they're pretty good people who need a little help from time to time, and that's what grace offers them. Some are like the elder brother in Jesus' parable of the prodigal.

> Jesus' offer of grace is staggering—and if we're not staggered by it, we haven't yet grasped it.

They give and serve, and they believe their obedience earns credit with God. They don't understand the biblical order of spiritual life: we don't obey to be accepted by God; we're accepted by his grace, a magnificent fact that motivates us to obey him from a full and overflowing heart. Over the years, the magnificent gift of salvation by grace through faith has been taught only as a ticket from hell to heaven. Deliverance from God's judgment is certainly a cornerstone of our faith, but the gospel is far richer, deeper, and more life-changing than that.

TURNAROUND

He was the most unlikely believer. In fact, when he told people he had come to faith in Jesus, no one believed him. His Jewish supporters couldn't imagine what he was saying, and the Christians were skeptical and thought it was a trick. He was an up-and-comer in the Jewish religious hierarchy, but something happened that completely turned his life around. Saul met Jesus.

In the earliest days after Jesus died, was raised, and ascended back to heaven, his followers in Jerusalem were the only established body of believers. Those who had come to the city for Pentecost and believed Peter's message had returned home. As believers spoke out about Christ, they experienced opposition from the same people who had felt threatened by Jesus.

Stephen had been appointed as one of the first deacons, but he wasn't content to manage the administrative tasks. He spoke out boldly about Jesus. In a repeat of what had happened to Jesus, he was arrested by the Jewish authorities and tried by the high priest. But unlike Jesus, he gave a long, impassioned defense of his faith, connecting the dots from Abraham to Joseph to Moses to Jesus. In quite a departure from Jesus' silence, Stephen didn't hedge his opinion. He told them, "You stiff-necked people, uncircumcised in heart and ears, you always resist the Holy Spirit. As your fathers did, so do you. Which of the prophets did your fathers not persecute? And they killed those who announced beforehand the coming of the Righteous One, whom you have now betrayed and murdered, you who received the law as delivered by angels and did not keep it" (Acts 7:51-53).

As you can imagine, the Jewish leaders were outraged and ordered that he be stoned to death. They took him outside, picked up rocks, and bludgeoned him. Saul served as a coat rack, approving every thud from the rocks that bounced off Stephen's body, leaving him broken and bloody. The anger of the Jewish leaders propelled them to try to stamp out the fledgling movement, and they launched a concerted persecution of the church. The believers were scattered, but they weren't shattered. They retained resilient faith. But one man took it upon himself to lead the persecution: Saul. He "was ravaging the church, and entering house after house, he dragged off men and women and committed them to prison" (Acts 8:3).

Saul didn't limit his efforts to Jerusalem. As the believers fled to other cities, he followed them. No one was safe. The high priest gave him introductory letters to explain to the synagogue leaders in Damascus that Saul was doing good work for him, so he took a search party with him to arrest believers in that city. The very last thing he expected was to meet Jesus on the way! Saul lost his sight, and Jesus told him to continue to Damascus. There, in one of the places in the Scriptures where we might see some humor, God told a man named Ananias to go to the house where Saul was staying to lay hands on him so he could regain his sight. Ananias was no fool. In effect, he said, "Uh, Lord, you may not know this, but Saul, the guy you want me to see, is a villain. He's come here to capture people . . . people like me! I'd like to pass on this one, if you don't mind." But God told Ananias, "Go, for he is a chosen instrument of mine to carry my name before the Gentiles and kings and the children of Israel. For I will show him how much he must suffer for the sake of my name" (Acts 9:15-16).

Saul became better known as Paul, and the rest of his life was a study in tenacious resilience. Jesus commissioned him to plant churches throughout the Roman world, and in virtually every city he was threatened—and sometimes physically beaten—after he told people about Jesus. For instance, below are a few examples from Paul's first (of three) missionary journeys. On this trip, he was traveling with Barnabas.

- In Pisidian Antioch, Paul was invited to speak in the synagogue. His message was well-received, prompting an invitation to come back the next week to tell even more people about Jesus. However, when the Jewish leaders saw the huge crowds of Gentiles ("almost the whole city") who had come to listen, they grew jealous and contradicted what Paul was telling the people. Paul and Barnabas were driven out of town (Acts 13:14-52).

+ In the next city, Iconium, Paul's preaching led to many Jews and Gentiles believing in Jesus, but those who didn't believe weren't content to merely engage in debate. When Paul discovered they had hatched a plot to stone him and Barnabas, they moved on (Acts 14:1-7).

+ The scene in Lystra is one of those that I'd love to see in the Instant Replay Room in heaven. After God used Paul to heal a crippled man, the pagan crowds who witnessed the miracle assumed Paul and Barnabas were gods. They brought out flowers and oxen to sacrifice to them. Paul pleaded for them to stop and told them about Jesus. They only reluctantly sent the livestock back to the fields. But a few days later, Paul's critics from Antioch and Iconium showed up, turned the crowd against him, and led them in stoning him, leaving him for dead. Miraculously, Paul woke up, got up, and went back into the city—talk about being resilient! The next day he and Barnabas went to Derbe where many people believed in Jesus (Acts 14:8-22).

We could look at many other specific moments when someone less motivated would have quit the project. In a catalog of the opposition he endured, Paul told the Corinthians that he had suffered . . .

. . . far greater labors, far more imprisonments, with countless beatings, and often near death. Five times I received at the hands of the Jews the forty lashes less one. Three times I was beaten with rods. Once I was stoned. Three times I was shipwrecked; a night and a day I was adrift at sea; on frequent journeys, in danger from rivers, danger from robbers, danger from my own people, danger from Gentiles, danger in the city, danger in the wilderness, danger at sea, danger from false brothers; in toil and hardship, through many a sleepless night, in hunger and thirst, often without food, in cold and exposure. And, apart from other things, there is the daily pressure on me of my anxiety for all the churches. Who is weak, and I am not weak? Who is made to fall, and I am not indignant? (2 Corinthians 11:23-29)

We might wonder what propelled Paul to keep going. A lot of people would have bailed out early when things were hard, but not Paul. He was empowered by the gospel. He had already told the church in Corinth what kept him going: "For the love of Christ controls us, because we have concluded this: that one has died for all, therefore all have died; and he died for all, that those who live might no longer live for themselves but for him who for their sake died and was raised" (2 Corinthians 5:14-15).

Every moment of Paul's life, every step he took, and every word he spoke and wrote were drenched in the gospel of grace. The gospel freed him, energized him, directed him, propelled him, and strengthened him all day every day. That's why Paul was so resilient. He put all of these truths together in his letter to Pastor Titus:

> The gospel freed him, energized him, directed him, propelled him, and strengthened him all day every day. That's why Paul was so resilient.

For the grace of God has appeared, bringing salvation for all people, training us to renounce ungodliness and worldly passions,
and to live self-controlled, upright, and godly lives in the present
age, waiting for our blessed hope, the appearing of the glory of
our great God and Savior Jesus Christ, who gave himself for us
to redeem us from all lawlessness and to purify for himself a
people for his own possession who are zealous for good works.
Declare these things; exhort and rebuke with all authority. Let
no one disregard you. (Titus 2:11-15)

Paul knew what awaited him in every city, but the love of Jesus was
more real to him than the bruises and scars on his body. Thankfully, few
of us are called to suffer like Paul, but all of us are called to let the gospel
permeate every aspect of our lives as we commit ourselves to proclaim
this amazing gospel of grace. The gospel has given us *freedom from* sin
and death, and it has given us *freedom to* live with integrity, kindness, and
generosity in our families, in our finances, and with our friends.

When we read Paul's letters to the churches and the pastors, we
notice that the gospel is stated or implied throughout each one. God's
love, forgiveness, acceptance, and power weren't aftermarket add-ons;
they're standard equipment for every believer. And with each reference
to the gospel, Paul reminds us of the source of our resilience. We aren't
resilient merely because of our moral rectitude, intellectual aptitude, or
internal fortitude. Spiritually speaking, we're resilient over our sinful past
only by the dynamic gospel of grace.

We get an intimate glimpse at Paul's heart when he met with the
Ephesian elders just prior to his return to Jerusalem to take an offering to
care for the poor in the city. The trip, he knew, wasn't going to be a vacation. He had spent three years in Ephesus, so he knew these elders very
well. He loved them and they loved him. He reminded them that they

had participated in his passion to share the gospel with everyone who would listen. He expected more suffering in Jerusalem, and he explained how he kept going even when pain was always on the horizon: "But I do not account my life of any value nor as precious to myself, if only I may finish my course and the ministry that I received from the Lord Jesus, to testify to the gospel of the grace of God" (Acts 20:24). He told them they wouldn't see him again, and then "he knelt down and prayed with them all. And there was much weeping on the part of all; they embraced Paul and kissed him, being sorrowful most of all because of the word he had spoken that they would not see him again" (vv. 36-38). For Paul, the gospel was the only thing that mattered because the gospel is all about Jesus.

We make a huge mistake if we believe Paul's life was just one problem after another . . . nothing but a grind day after day. The grace of God lifted his spirit, filled his heart with gratitude, and infused him with great joy. To him, the sacrifice of personal comfort to achieve true purpose, seeing lives changed, and being Jesus' partner was well worth the trade-off.

Paul's letter to the Philippians is a thank-you note for their generosity in supporting him and his ministry. Though he was in prison when he wrote it, joy gushes throughout each passage. He tells them he has joy when he prays for them because they blessed him with their generous gifts. He reveals the startling news that he doesn't know if he'll live much longer, but he's comforted by their spiritual growth and their own joy in following Jesus. He shares that he has great joy because they are living according to the gospel, experiencing encouragement, comfort, love, and the power of the Holy Spirit. In perhaps the most personal and poignant part of the letter, Paul relates how some people were trying to derail his ministry and cloud his message, but nothing can stop him. He writes that nothing—absolutely nothing—can compete with the joy and power that Jesus gives:

But whatever gain I had, I counted as loss for the sake of Christ. Indeed, I count everything as loss because of the surpassing worth of knowing Christ Jesus my Lord. For his sake I have suffered the loss of all things and count them as rubbish, in order that I may gain Christ and be found in him, not having a righteousness of my own that comes from the law, but that which comes through faith in Christ, the righteousness from God that depends on faith—that I may know him and the power of his resurrection, and may share his sufferings, becoming like him in his death. (Philippians 3:7-10)

Near the end of this letter, Paul encourages them to "Rejoice in the Lord always; again I will say, rejoice," and he promises "the peace of God, which surpasses all understanding" (4:4, 7). At that point, he connects some very important dots in the letter. He tells them, "Finally, brothers, whatever is true, whatever is honorable, whatever is just, whatever is pure, whatever is lovely, whatever is commendable, if there is any excellence, if there is anything worthy of praise, think about these things" (v. 8). Earlier, he had included a poem or a song about the humility, sacrifice, and exaltation of Christ, so here, he's saying, "Focus your thoughts on the one who is the Truth, who is Honor personified, who brings justice to the oppressed, who is sinless and holy, is more beautiful than anything we can imagine, is the focus of our attention, whose every attribute is perfect and immeasurable, and is supremely worthy of praise." Paul is pointing them (and us) to Jesus and his gospel.

Jesus wasn't an addendum to Paul's life; he was front and center (Philippians 1:21). In fact, nothing else came close, and he considered everything that might compete with the priority of Jesus as, well, trash. As we've seen, we're drawn toward lesser things, things that promise to give us ultimate meaning but leave us empty. The lure of popularity, power, possessions, and prestige is incredibly strong, but Jesus' love is stronger. Jesus gives us transcendent joy.

CENTER POINT

It's human nature to see ourselves as the center of the universe, and everyone and everything revolves around our wishes. A corollary to that perspective is that our performance somehow earns God's approval. Yes, there are plenty of commands in the New Testament, and yes, we're to take them seriously . . . but they're not the basis of our acceptance with God! When we think we're more loved and more loveable because we're more disciplined, more obedient, more faithful, more generous, or more of anything else, we step onto the soul-numbing treadmill of superiority and inferiority. When we're doing well (defined as better than someone else), we feel good about ourselves, better than others, and completely justified in condemning "those people" who aren't as disciplined, obedient, etc. But when we mess up and we don't measure up to the standards, we feel inferior. We call ourselves horrible names, and we grovel in self-pity. Neither arrogance nor self-pity is listed among the fruit of the Spirit!

Believing that our good performance earns points with God puts us again in the center of the universe because it's up to us to make life work, to do everything it takes to earn God's approval. We've looked at the gospel message in Ephesians 2, but we stopped at verse 9. It's instructive to read the next verse: "For we are his workmanship, created in Christ Jesus for good works, which God prepared beforehand, that we should walk in them" (v. 10).

We're created by God and we live for God. It's all about him, not us. Why do we do good works in obedience to God? Later in the letter, Paul paints a beautiful and powerful picture: "Therefore be imitators of God, as beloved children. And walk in love, as Christ loved us and gave himself up for us, a fragrant offering and sacrifice to God" (5:1-2). A child who is dearly loved delights in obeying his parents. Love is the most powerful motivator, and we are the recipients of Jesus' sweet smelling sacrifice—his perfect, sacrificial love.

Is Jesus a lovely aroma to you? Is he beautiful? Those who are overwhelmed with grace find him beautiful, but those who haven't yet grasped the wonder of his grace expect him to be useful: to meet their needs, make their lives pleasant, and take away their troubles. That's not a life based on the gospel. It's something far less.

When we understand the gospel message to be "receive Jesus into your life," I think we miss the comprehensive call for the gospel to penetrate every goal, every relationship, and every choice. I believe it's more accurate to use the phrase "release your life to Jesus." This is, I'm convinced, language that fits Paul's understanding that the gospel is a free gift that costs us nothing but cost Jesus everything. It's only reasonable, then, to give him everything we are, everything we have, and everything we hope for the future. In his book, *Finding God*, author Larry Crabb observes that many people treat Jesus like "a specially attentive waiter" rather than their all-powerful, infinitely loving King. When we get good service from him, we give him a tip of praise; when we don't get what we think we deserve, we complain.[31]

Paul fell hard from his perch as a rising star among the Jewish leaders, but at the bottom, he found grace. In his letter to the Christians in Galatia, he had to correct their misguided thinking (based on faulty teaching from outsiders) that they had to earn God's acceptance by following particular rules. Legalism and moralism create bondage, but grace sets us free—not free to sin all we want, but free to follow Jesus without the burden of guilt and shame. Near the end of this letter, Paul explained that his adversaries, the ones who advocated strict adherence to rules to earn acceptance from God, couldn't actually deal with the underlying problem of sin. Paul contrasted their boast in legalistic obedience with his boast that Jesus' death is all we need: "But far be it from me to boast except in the cross of our Lord Jesus Christ, by which the world has been crucified to me, and I to the world" (Galatians 6:14). In this way, identifying with Christ's death is the doorway to true life.

Our sinful passions died with Christ on the cross, and we live with the same power that raised Jesus from the grave. We can be *proponents* of grace by letting the love of Jesus transform us from the inside out, or we can be *opponents* of grace by insisting that following rules is all God wants from us. I'm going with Option A. How about you?

THINK ABOUT IT:

1. Do you know anyone who has felt condemned by people in the church? How did it affect that person?

2. How would you define and describe "moralistic therapeutic deism"? Why do you think it's popular with so many people? What are some ways it misses the gospel?

3. How do you explain Paul's tenacious resilience to represent Jesus wherever he went? Is his commitment attractive to you? Why or why not?

4. As you've read about Paul in the past, did you see him as a joyful person? What might it look like for you to be both radically committed and thoroughly joyful because of the gospel?

5. What are some signs someone views God as "a specially attentive waiter"?

6. Do you find Jesus to be beautiful, or useful? Explain your answer.

7. What difference would it make for you to grasp the gospel even more deeply and clearly?

Affirmation:

Jesus' offer of grace is staggering—and if we're not staggered by it, we haven't yet grasped it.

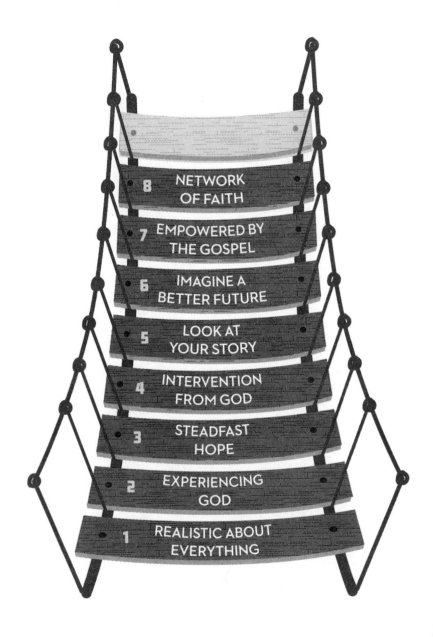

8 NETWORK OF FAITH

7 EMPOWERED BY THE GOSPEL

6 IMAGINE A BETTER FUTURE

5 LOOK AT YOUR STORY

4 INTERVENTION FROM GOD

3 STEADFAST HOPE

2 EXPERIENCING GOD

1 REALISTIC ABOUT EVERYTHING

CHAPTER 8

NETWORK OF FAITH

Ultimate reality is a community of persons who know
and love one another. That is what the universe, God,
history, and life is all about. If you favor money, power,
and accomplishment over human relationships, you will
dash yourself on the rocks of reality.

—*Tim Keller*

There's a famous saying that "If you want to go fast, go alone. If you want to go far, go together." The next plank on the bridge to resilience is a *network of faith*.

My adolescent and young adult years were, to be honest, odd. I started preaching when I was sixteen. While my peers were hanging out and having fun, I was in the church office; when they were wearing the latest styles, I wore a suit to be presentable to the people in the church. I felt strongly that God was calling me to this role, but I also felt different . . . isolated . . . lonely. I didn't have a wealth of experience to teach me the important lessons of life and leadership, so I needed to find some people who would support me and speak into my life.

Deacon Larry Martin, Mother Betty Stanford, and Mother George pastored me even though I was their pastor. They didn't have a pastoral title, but they lovingly walked with me through good times and bad. They supported and encouraged me when I made good decisions, and they treated me with grace when I made immature ones.

When my marriage fell apart, they "preached" the message of vulnerability, courage, resilience, grace, and love to me. They loved me enough to tell me the truth and help me wrestle with hard choices. After I told our deacons that I was getting a divorce, Deacon Martin met with me, opened his Bible, and read, "God hates divorce." He wasn't pulling any punches, and he wasn't winking at my failures; however, his tone and demeanor told me that he wasn't condemning me. He was sharing what God's Word says and opening a dialogue. After we talked for a while, he said, "Pastor, I can't make your decision for you. All I can do is share my convictions. No matter what decision you make, God hasn't changed his heart toward you. His love doesn't stop. It's unconditional." He paused for a few seconds, and then added, "Pastor, there's nothing you can do to make God love you any more, and there's nothing you can do to make him love you any less." (It was, as you may recall, the message I gave the unwed mother when we met in the mall atrium. It stuck with me then, and it always will.) That moment with Deacon Martin was a shining demonstration of the undeserved and unconditional love of God.

On the first Sunday in August, right after I'd announced to the deacons that my wife and I were getting a divorce, our church held communion, the Lord's Supper. I officiated the meal, but I didn't partake of it. Instead, I decided to tell the congregation about my failed marriage. I'm not sure why I thought that was a good time for the announcement. My thinking must have been clouded by the swirl of intense emotions, but I pressed on and began telling them the painful news. However, after a few sentences, I broke down and sobbed uncontrollably. Mother Betty Stanford and Deacon Larry Martin both rose from their seats, walked up to the pulpit, one standing on my right and the other on my left, with their arms enveloping me with a nearly suffocating hug. It meant so much to me because I felt so terribly alone and condemned. They leaned over, whispered a prayer in my ear, and then said, "Pastor, it's going to be okay. It's going to be okay."

Far too often, people speak the truth to blast and manipulate, or on the other end of the spectrum, they define love as never saying anything that might challenge anyone's presumptions. Jesus came "full of grace and truth," and that's the way these people treated me. I sometimes wonder what the trajectory of my life might have been if those dear people hadn't loved me so well at a time when I felt utterly unlovable. Thankfully, it's only a thought, not a reality. Love covers a multitude of sins . . . even mine.

SURPRISING TENDERNESS

When you think of the apostle Paul, what comes to mind? Many of us see him as the ultimate tough guy, the man who would run through a brick wall to accomplish his goals, who never stopped, who overcame enormous obstacles by sheer force of will. I've heard people say, "I'd love to spend time with Jesus, but Paul? He scares me to death!" However, when we look a little more closely at his life, we see someone whose passion for Jesus and the gospel filtered down into his genuine love for people.

As we've seen, Paul faced opposition in virtually every city and town where he traveled. In Philippi, the new church included Lydia, who was a wealthy businesswoman, a slave girl who had been freed from a demon, and the jailer, who had almost certainly been a Roman soldier, along with his family. We talk about diversity, but this is beyond anything we normally imagine! This fledgling group of believers with their varying backgrounds all loved Paul and supported him. When he was again in prison, this time in Rome, he wrote back to thank them for their help. He explained that, paradoxically, the gospel was spreading faster because he was in prison: "Most of the brothers, having become confident in the Lord by my imprisonment, are much more bold to speak the word without fear" (Philippians 1:14). Paul's confidence in his future was a product of two forces: the *intervention* of the Spirit and the *intercession* of the saints: "for I know that through your prayers and the help of the Spirit of Jesus Christ this will turn out for my deliverance" (v. 19).

In a section of the letter that's often overlooked, we see the tenderness of Paul toward two men he loved. Timothy had become a son in the faith, a close friend, and a partner in ministry. Paul told the Philippians that he planned to send Timothy to them, and we get a glimpse of his heart for the young man: "For I have no one like him, who will be genuinely concerned for your welfare. For they all seek their own interests, not those of Jesus Christ. But you know Timothy's proven worth, how as a son with a father he has served with me in the gospel" (Philippians 2:20-22). Then, Paul shares what has been going on with another dear friend, Epaphroditus, who had been sent by the Philippians to care for Paul. Epaphroditus became seriously ill, and Paul knew that everyone—including himself—would be devastated if he didn't recover: "For he has been longing for you all and has been distressed because you heard that he was ill. Indeed he was ill, near to death. But God had mercy on him, and not only on him but on me also, lest I should have sorrow upon sorrow. I am the more eager to send him, therefore, that you may rejoice at seeing him again, and that I may be less anxious" (vv. 26-28). Tough guy? Yes, in some ways, but with a tender heart.

> Tough guy? Yes, in some ways, but with a tender heart.

PARTNERS

The letter to the Philippians gives us insights into Paul's love for people, and as we look at Luke's account of Paul's life in Acts and read more of his letters, an even clearer picture emerges. After Paul met Jesus on the road to Damascus, he soon went on an extended sabbatical to Arabia to study, think, and pray. This is likely when Jesus revealed to him truths about the gospel that made him so confident that the Messiah was far more than a human military leader (Galatians 1:11-12). After three years, he went back to Damascus to preach that Jesus is the Christ, but in a preview of what was to come, he had to flee for his life. He traveled south to Jerusalem to meet with church leaders, and then he went home to Tarsus for more study and preparation for ministry. After perhaps nine or ten years, Barnabas, one of the leaders of the church, went to Tarsus to find Paul. The two men went to Antioch on the Syrian coast, which had become one of the leading centers of the church after many were forced to flee persecution in Jerusalem. The two men were commissioned by the church to make a missionary journey to what is now central Turkey. They decided to take a young man, John Mark, with them, but soon after they started, John Mark got cold feet and returned home.

Barnabas, whose name means "son of encouragement," was exactly that for Paul on his first major ministry venture. Paul preached boldly in every city, usually first to the Jews in the synagogues to connect the dots between Jewish prophecy and Jesus, but when they didn't listen, Paul preached to the Gentiles.

When Paul and Barnabas returned to Antioch, they reported the startling news that Gentiles who believed showed the same signs of salvation as the believing Jews! They were equal in the new body of Christ-believers! Some Jewish Christians couldn't wrap their minds around the thought of equality with Gentiles; they strongly believed that Gentiles had to become Jewish before they could be Christians. In one of the most important meetings in church history, the church's leaders in Jerusalem heard both sides and pronounced the inclusion of believing Gentiles into the church. Paul was the chief spokesman for the cause—the same man who had pledged his life to destroy the Christian faith a few years before—and Barnabas was his partner, support system, and dear friend.

Their partnership, though, became strained as they made plans for their second gospel mission trip. Barnabas wanted to take John Mark again, but Paul wasn't willing. After what must have been an intense argument, the two men separated. Silas took Barnabas's place on the two-man team while Barnabas went to minister elsewhere with John Mark (Acts 15:36-41). Paul and Silas made it all the way to Europe: to Philippi, Athens, and Corinth, picking up young Timothy along the way as they traveled to Antioch by way of Ephesus.

On a third long trip, Paul stayed for three years in Ephesus, one of the leading cities in the Roman Empire. There, he built strong relationships, but his preaching eventually caused a riot. Again, he traveled to Greece before returning to Jerusalem. On this trip, he was joined by another companion, Luke, who had a firsthand account for the rest of his history of the early church. Luke stayed with Paul throughout his arrest in Jerusalem, lengthy imprisonment in Caesarea, and transfer to Rome, including a harrowing shipwreck during a storm. Luke was also a witness to Paul's welcome by believers in Rome even as he was under house arrest.

As Paul wrote letters to the churches, he graciously credited his companions in the bylines. For instance, Timothy is included in the salutations of several letters. One of the most interesting facts about Paul's strong connections with people is the restoration of his relationship with John Mark. As Paul neared the end of his life, he wrote his final letter to Timothy. He asked his young friend to come for a visit because he was lonely. Luke was with him, but Demas, a member of his team, had deserted him, and he had sent another on a mission trip. In the conclusion of his last letter, Paul wrote, "Get Mark and bring him with you, for he is very useful to me for ministry" (2 Timothy 4:11).

We experience frictions in our friendships and ruptures in our relationships, but grace can reweave the torn fabric of our connections and make them stronger than before. The restoration of strained or broken relationships is a beautiful thing, but we need to be clear-eyed about it. Ignoring the difficulty isn't resolution. For genuine restoration to take place, both parties need to admit their part in the problem, each one needs to enter the pain the other has suffered to show empathy, and each one needs to make a commitment to resolve problems in the future before they metastasize into a crisis. Forgiveness is unilateral—we are called by God to forgive whether the other person ever apologizes or changes—but reconciliation always requires both people to take steps to repent, to understand, and to speak the truth with love. We can't make other people reconcile with us. We can offer a path and see who will join us, but sadly, some simply won't. When this happens, we grieve, but there's no need for any guilt. We've done what we could do, and we've let the other person make his or her decision. Forgiveness frees us from being consumed by resentment. When we forgive, we release the person from our heart's prison, and we find that we're released from prison, too.

> We experience frictions in our friendships and ruptures in our relationships, but grace can reweave the torn fabric of our connections and make them stronger than before.

EMOJI WORLD

The depth and quality of relationships is, of course, based on the depth and quality of communication. My next comment may brand me as completely out of touch with the modern world, but if that's the case, so be it. Here it is: As I look at today's culture, I'm astonished at the sheer magnitude of information communicated with staggering shallowness. In the blink of the historical eye, we've gone from writing letters and trea-suring intimate conversations to quick social media posts and a zillion emojis in response. The Pew Research Center study reported that just five percent of American adults used social media in 2005, but today, about three-fourths of adults use these platforms.[32] If the quality of our communication kept up with the quantity, it would be wonderful, but it hasn't. Research shows an inverse relationship between social media and intimate communication because people post things online they'd never say face-to-face. Social media has been linked to increased interpersonal conflict, a rise in feelings of jealousy, and the inability to move on after a breakup because "checking up on an ex's profile led to more distress over the breakup, more negative feelings, and less personal growth."[33]

Social media is all about the clicks, and nothing gets clicks like out-rage and anger. Eighty-six percent of American adults get news online, including sixty percent who use these platforms exclusively.[34] The prob-lem is that the news is curated by people who have a vested interest in hooking people and bringing them back again and again. How do they do that? It's simple and insidious: sites use algorithms to select the specific kind of feeds to send our way, feeds that pour gasoline on the fires of our fear and hate. The grand expectation that social media would lead to stronger, more intimate connections has proven false. Instead, the plat-forms have created "filter bubbles" that reinforce what we already believe (or fear). In a *Forbes* article titled "Is Social Media Curating Hate and Scouring the Web for Our Greatest Fears?", the author observes:

> ... perhaps most troubling, concerns are increasingly being raised about the nature of this echo chamber and whether instead of surrounding us with things we like and make us happy, those social algorithms are ensuring we are deluged with hate and our deepest and darkest fears in order to maintain us in a state of

perpetual fear and anger that will maximize our likelihood of consuming and engaging with content and producing our own responses in turn. . . .

A post filled with hate and vitriol might prompt us to fire off a barrage of counter-posts condemning it, forward it widely to others asking them to condemn it and countless side conversations about how someone could harbor such horrific views and what it means about the state of the world.[35]

In the endless search for meaning and happiness, we've settled for hate and fear. Over the years, numerous studies have polled people about what makes them happy. If we look at the ads online, on television, or in magazines, we'd conclude that what really matters is wealth, beautiful skin, gorgeous clothes, a new car, or a fabulous vacation, but we'd be wrong. Again and again, the studies show that people desperately want a few close relationships. Christian psychologists Les and Leslie Parrott observe: "Nothing reaches so deeply into the human personality, tugs so tightly, as relationship. Why? For one reason, it is only in the context of connection with others that our deepest needs can be met. Whether we like it or not, each of us has an unshakable dependence on others. It's what philosopher John Donne was getting at when he said so succinctly, 'No man is an island.' We need camaraderie, affection, love. These are not options in life, or sentimental trimmings; they are part of our species' survival kit. We *need* to belong."[36]

A TRUE FRIEND

I think we give John Mark a raw deal. How many of us would have stuck by Paul when crowds turned against him and he was beaten, stoned, and whipped? It would have been completely understandable if we told him, "Hey, Paul, it's been a lot of fun, but it's time for me to go home.

You'll be fine. I just know it." That was John Mark's response, and Demas also bailed out on Paul, but plenty of others stuck with him through thick and thin. They were true friends.

I want to turn to another remarkable friendship. As we've seen, the prophet Samuel anointed David as the new king of Israel, but Saul was already on the throne. I'm not sure when Saul became certifiably crazy, but after David received public praise for killing Goliath, Saul became enraged and tried to kill him. As we've seen, David had a surprising ally, Jonathan, Saul's son, who was the rightful heir. The historian gives us a peek at one scene. David and his mighty men had been running for their lives for some time, but again, they escaped. "When Saul was told that David had escaped from Keilah, he gave up the expedition. And David remained in the strongholds in the wilderness, in the hill country of the wilderness of Ziph. And Saul sought him every day, but God did not give him into his hand" (1 Samuel 23:13-14).

David was in big trouble, and he didn't know how long he could last in the desert. Then . . . "Jonathan, Saul's son, rose and went to David at Horesh, and strengthened his hand in God. And he said to him, 'Do not fear, for the hand of Saul my father shall not find you. You shall be king over Israel, and I shall be next to you. Saul my father also knows this.' And the two of them made a covenant before the Lord. David remained at Horesh, and Jonathan went home" (vv. 16-18).

In this passage, we can see four principles of life-changing friendships:

1. Jonathan entered David's experience.

He didn't stay in the palace in comfort and splendor, he didn't think he was too good to get his hands dirty, and he didn't just say, "I'll pray for you." Jonathan went into the wilderness of Ziph to be with David.

2. Jonathan had empathy for David's condition.

He knew that his father saw David as a threat and wanted to kill him, but he risked his own life to show compassion for his friend. Showing up isn't enough. Real friends build resilience because they demonstrate a caring heart. We see a contrast between Jonathan and Job's friends: they heard about his calamites and showed up, but their misperceptions and false accusations piled more pain on Job.

3. Jonathan wasn't envious of David's elevation.

To be sure, David's anointing—his right to become king—hadn't yet been realized, but Jonathan wasn't looking for way to hold on to power. Instead, he offered his assurance that David would be the next king in Israel. When a friend receives a promotion or an award, it's human nature for us to compare and be jealous, but true friends celebrate as much for another's success as for their own.

4. Jonathan encouraged David to endure.

In fact, they made an iron-clad commitment to each other. I'm not sure why either of them could have wondered about the other's commitment, but the threat level was so high that they decided to make a solemn, binding covenant. As a wedding ceremony is the public declaration of the couple's bond, the covenant between David and Jonathan gave them a moment they could look back on and say, "No matter what happens, we're in this together."

We might assume that only a few people have "the right personality" for deep, lasting friendships, but that's not true. Certainly, personality and temperament play a role, but God has made all of us with two essential ingredients: the *capacity* to develop friendships and the *need* for them. We simply can't be the people God wants us to be without genuine connections with others. Some are extroverts and others are introverts—that doesn't mean the first group has friends and the second doesn't. It means they relate to their friends in different ways. Extroverts have a lot of friends, and they're always glad to add a few more; introverts treasure a few friends, and they're cautious about adding more to the mix. Some are planners and organizers, so they're happy to be in charge of a weekend trip, but others are more spontaneous and free-spirited. Some are laid-back, and others thrive on more intense conversations. The point is that we all bring something to the table, and we all have needs that others can meet. Friends *step in* when times are hard, and they *step up* to celebrate our successes—and quite often, they're a lot more fun to be around than family members. After all, as the saying goes, "Friends are the family we get to choose for ourselves."

RESILIENT RELATIONSHIPS

In God's forever family, we're called to have strong, honest, loving relationships so that we encourage each other to deepen our grasp of grace, hold people accountable to walk in truth, and be light and salt to the world. In Paul's letters, we see the struggles he faced as he planted churches. The Corinthians were notoriously prideful and contentious, so Paul went into great detail to explain how the body of Christ functions in both unity of heart and a diversity of talents. Some of the believers in Thessalonica were sure Jesus had already come back, and they were left behind. (Talk about a rumor that will ruin your day!) And the Philippians, who began with amazing diversity and loyalty to God and Paul, had to wrestle with conflict between two prominent women of the church. Even the sweeping, grand letters to the Ephesians (which was a circular letter to a number of churches) and Romans (which is the richest theological treatise ever penned) applied the message of the gospel to nuts and bolts, everyday relationships in the family, at work, and in the church. We can draw a conclusion from these letters: people grow, mature, serve, and reach the lost only when they're in resilient relationships with one another.

Paul's letters are rich and instructive, but we also have an outsider's perspective on the kind of relationships among Christians in the early church. Lucian of Samosata was a Greek pagan writer who lived in the middle of the second century, during the time of severe persecution of Christians and the first of the great plagues that swept through the Roman Empire. He carefully observed how Christians acted . . . and how their actions were so different from the rest of the culture. He wrote:

> People grow, mature, serve, and reach the lost only when they're in resilient relationships with one another.

> The Christians, you know, worship a man to this day—the distinguished personage who introduced their novel rites, and was crucified on that account. . . . You see, these misguided creatures start with the general conviction that they are immortal for all time, which explains the contempt of death and voluntary self-devotion which are so common among them; and then it was impressed on them by their original lawgiver that they are all brothers, from the moment that they are converted, and deny the gods of Greece, and worship the crucified sage, and live after his laws. All this they take quite on faith, with the result that they despise all worldly goods alike, regarding them merely as common property.[37]

The Christian faith thrived, even in the face of opposition and ridicule, because believers loved each other so much that they gladly gave themselves and their possessions to those in need. How are we doing today? The culture is more polarized than ever before. People don't just *disagree* about policies and ideas—they *hate* those who disagree with them! And tragically, we can't just write them off as pagans and unbelievers because we see similar divisions in the church. (And we thought the Corinthians were a fractured church!) We fight about politics and racism, and these arguments spill over into debates about economic opportunity and equality, as well as how we treat immigrants, the poor, and anyone else considered to be "them." The umbrella of the kingdom of Jesus is big enough for people of every race, every political party, every socioeconomic group, and every nationality, but only if we treasure Jesus more than our personal and political ambitions. That's the friction point.

> The Christian faith thrived, even in the face of opposition and ridicule, because believers loved each other so much that they gladly gave themselves and their possessions to those in need. How are we doing today?

We're at a point in our culture and in our churches that far too many people treat Jesus like a weapon of political power instead of a Savior and King we bow humbly before. Theologians and avid readers of the Bible often identify "the hard sayings of Jesus," but they're necessary for us to grasp if we want to be resilient. One of these is found in three of the Gospels. It may seem to be a strange passage for ending this chapter, but bear with me. Jesus had just told the disciples that he was going to suffer, die, and be raised from the dead, but that wasn't in Peter's plan. He couldn't imagine how the Messiah, Israel's king, could conquer the Romans if he was dead! Peter tried to correct Jesus, but Jesus told him, "Get behind me, Satan! For you are not setting your mind on the things of God, but on the things of man" (Mark 8:33). Jesus then takes the opportunity to apply the principle more broadly:

> And calling the crowd to him with his disciples, he said to them, "If anyone would come after me, let him deny himself and take up his cross and follow me. For whoever would save his life will lose it, but whoever loses his life for my sake and the gospel's will save it. For what does it profit a man to gain the whole world and forfeit his soul? For what can a man give in return for his soul? (vv. 34-37)

Isn't that the message we need to hear and follow today? As long as we have our minds set on "the things of man," we'll miss God's heart, create division instead of unity, and despise instead of loving those who disagree with us, annoy us, or look different than us. The task in the second century was for believers to say "no" to their selfishness and reach out to care for each other in a time of persecution and plague . . . and that's how they became resilient. Today, our situation may be different, but the directive is the same: to say "no" to our selfishness, our insistence on our rights, and the adrenaline rush of hate, and replace those with a listening ear, a helping hand, and a loving heart. That's losing our lives for Jesus' sake . . . that's finding and saving a meaningful life. That's what resilience looks like in our churches, our offices, our homes, and our neighborhoods. That's the foundation of honest, trusting, soul-nourishing friendships.

THINK ABOUT IT:

1. Have you ever needed a friend but couldn't find one? If so, how did that make you feel?

2. When has someone stepped into your life "full of grace and truth"? What difference did it make for you? (Or if this hasn't been your experience, what difference do you think it might have made when you were struggling?)

3. Paul was a very intense, driven person. How would you describe his closest partnerships and friendships?

4. What is the evidence that social media algorithms are designed to feed our outrage and our fears? How can you tell if you're being affected? What will it take to change your involvement so you're more objective and hopeful?

5. Look again at the four principles from the friendship of Jonathan and David. Which of those do you do well? Describe your impact of those strengths on others. And which of them need a little improvement? What would progress look like?

6. What are some ways Jesus' call to lose our lives so we can find real life apply to our relationships in the church and outside it?

Affirmation:

People grow, mature, serve, and reach the lost only when they're in resilient relationships with one another.

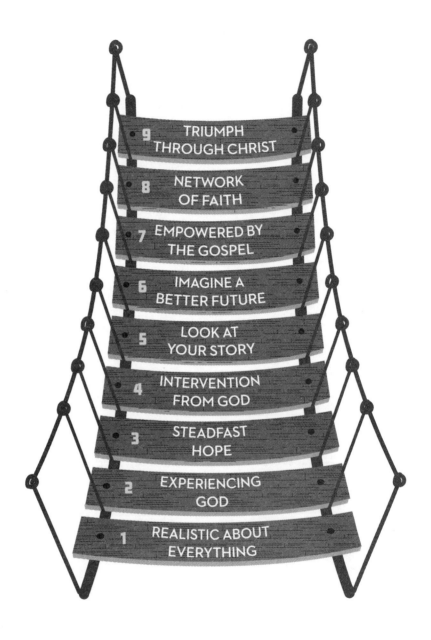

CHAPTER 9

TRIUMPH THROUGH CHRIST

*What do you do with a man who is supposed to be the
holiest man who has ever lived and yet goes around
talking with prostitutes and hugging lepers? What do
you do with a man who not only mingles with the most
unsavory people but actually seems to enjoy them?
The religious accused him of being a drunkard, a glutton
and having tacky taste in friends. It is a profound irony
that the Son of God visited this planet and one of
the chief complaints against him was that he
was not religious enough.*
— Rebecca Manley Pippert

No one is beyond hope. No one is outside the reach of God's love. No one is so far gone that it's impossible to come back to God and experience the wonder of forgiveness, hope, and purpose. Are you ready to complete your bridge to resilience? The last plank is our *triumph through Christ.*

In my years as a pastor, I've never seen anything that compares to "the year of the pandemic." I've been challenged to respond to the full range of difficulties in the lives of our people: sickness, death, doubt, despair, financial hardship, food shortage, and all the rest. This experience has reshaped the lives of the people in our church, and it has reshaped my conception of my role as a pastor. I've discovered that T. D. Jakes was right when he said, "I found that the things that hurt us the most can become the fuel and the catalyst that propel us toward our destiny. It will either make you bitter or it will make you better."

In fact, not long before I sat down to work on this chapter, I had a conversation with the director of our Christian counseling ministry. She told me about the deaths of eleven people who are either in our church or are related to our people. The deceased are fathers and mothers, sisters and brothers, sons and daughters, aunts and uncles, and they have left a gaping hole in their families. I asked the director to set up video calls with the eleven families, and I finished those conversations just minutes ago. One of the ladies asked me to officiate in the funeral for her sister, but her present grief is compounded by the death of her mother in the early months of the pandemic and her godmother just weeks ago.

As I've received news about people who have gotten so sick they've been hospitalized, I've had to cope with the fact that I couldn't go to see them to give them comfort and hope. It breaks my heart that many of those people died alone. Jesus was present, certainly, but the touch and words of their families and their pastor were missing. Certainly, the overflowing compassion of nurses and doctors has been amazing, but it's not the same as having the people who love you by your side in your final days, hours, and minutes.

> Like churches throughout the world, the people in our congregation have battled with uncertainty and grief.

Like churches throughout the world, the people in our congregation have battled with uncertainty and grief. One lady has lost her mother, an aunt, and a brother to the disease. She told me, "Pastor, I've been in a Life Group for a while, but I never understood the value of these supportive relationships until this past year. I don't know what I would have done without these people. Their love, their calls, and their prayers have strengthened me, and through them, God has given me a peace that passes all understanding." She continued, "I've heard you teach and preach about God's peace many times over the years, but this is the first time I've actually experienced it. My heart is still hurting. I still cry, but my faith is firmly anchored in Christ."

During the pandemic, my focus has shifted. Before the calendar turned to 2020, I spent a lot of time organizing events for our five campuses, training leaders, and planning for the future. When we stopped having services and our people started suffering and dying, I quickly realized my role was to be exclusively their shepherd, to comfort the afflicted and point people to Jesus as the solid center in the middle of the problems swirling around them. For our people and for me, the real triumph isn't a growing church or constructing a pleasant life. There's nothing wrong with those goals, as long as we see them as gifts from God. But the real triumph is knowing, loving, and following Jesus. His path may lead us into places we don't really want to go, but we can be sure he's with us there. If we're on a walk with a guide on a sunny day, we might wander off to sightsee, but if we're out on an unfamiliar trail on a stormy night, we grab our guide's arm and hold on tight. Many of us, including me, have been holding tight to Jesus as we've been pounded by the nighttime storm of the season of Covid. Holding his arm doesn't make the storm stop, but it gives us confidence, hope, and yes, a peace that passes all understanding because we trust that he is far wiser, far more powerful, and far more loving than we could ever imagine. And he can see in the dark. Trusting him is the secret of a resilient life.

IN THE PARADE

To walk with Christ—and let the wonder of grace permeate every aspect of our lives—is our greatest challenge and our highest joy. Some of us have grown up in a revivalist tradition that emphasized the moment of salvation, and redemption wasn't followed up with sound teaching about how to grow in our faith. The gospel, though, is far more than just a ticket out of hell. When we trust in Jesus, we're saying, "You're my Savior, and you're also my King. I'm yours—body, soul, and spirit." This transformation isn't just for nice people to become a little nicer; it's for the hopeless to find hope and outcasts to be adopted into God's family. As we've seen, the Corinthians were a motley bunch. They fought, were jealous, and had to have love defined for them because they were so far from it. But God worked in their hearts and transformed their behavior. Paul's first letter to them is corrective, but his second letter has a very different tone. Early in it he responds to the news that they had repented, and he wrote them:

> But thanks be to God, who in Christ always leads us in triumphal procession, and through us spreads the fragrance of the knowledge of him everywhere. For we are the aroma of Christ to God among those who are being saved and among those who are perishing, to one a fragrance from death to death, to the other a fragrance from life to life. Who is sufficient for these things? For we are not, like so many, peddlers of God's word, but as men of sincerity, as commissioned by God, in the sight of God we speak in Christ. (2 Corinthians 2:14-17)

When Roman emperors and generals came from military victories, they entered Rome behind a long parade of soldiers and conquered people. Paul is comparing that scene with Christ's victory over sin and death, but the parade isn't the end for us. We become his partners to share the sweet love of Jesus with everyone, those in the family of God and those we hope will join the family. We haven't earned this privilege. It's a gift. And we don't use it for personal gain—we're God's people who are his partners in the family business, representing him with love, compassion, integrity, and hope.

How does this work? What happens in us that changes us so dramatically? In the letter to the Galatians, Paul explains that profound theological truth transforms our identity, our motivations, and the trajectory of our lives . . . and of course, it's all about grace. He explained, "We also have believed in Christ Jesus, in order to be justified by faith in Christ and not by works of the law, because by works of the law no one will be justified" (Galatians 2:16).

Justification has two parts: Christ's death is imputed to us to pay for all of our sins, so we're forgiven, and Christ's perfect life is imputed to us so we're declared righteous. As we've seen, we can't earn it, we don't deserve it, but it's a free gift. Jesus identified with us by becoming a human being, and in our response to the gospel, we identify with him. Paul explained, "I have been crucified with Christ. It is no longer I who live, but Christ who lives in me. And the life I now live in the flesh I live by faith in the Son of God, who loved me and gave himself for me. I do not nullify the grace of God, for if righteousness were through the law, then Christ died for no purpose" (vv. 20-21). This is the wonder of our new relationship with God—our selfish deeds and desires have been nailed to the cross and paid for, and the Spirit of God

> We receive God's love by grace through faith, and God changes us from the inside out so we want to obey the one who loves us so much.

has taken up residence in us. As we grow in our faith, selfishness subsides and we gradually take on more of Christ's heart and values. We receive God's love by grace through faith, and God changes us from the inside out so we want to obey the one who loves us so much.

IN THE STORM

Self-reliance is considered a strength . . . until it's not enough. Sooner or later, all of us come to a point when our intelligence, skills, and experience can't get us out of a quagmire of trouble. It happens to us, and it happened to the disciples. Mark's account of the life of Christ paints a particular picture of calamity and hopelessness. After Jesus had taught the crowds, he and the disciples got into a boat, and he instructed them to sail to the other side of the Sea of Galilee. Jesus was exhausted from all the teaching, and he went to sleep.

Fierce winds could blow from the surrounding hills to the sea far below, creating sudden and violent storms. One of these storms began to batter the disciples' boat with waves, and it began to fill with water. At least four of the men were trained, experienced fishermen who had spent their adult lives in boats on the sea, but even they panicked. They woke Jesus (He must have been really tired to sleep through all this!), and barked at him, "Teacher, do you not care that we are perishing?" It was a desperate plea for help. Jesus woke up, got up, and spoke up. He said to the sea, "Peace! Be still!" (Mark 4:35-41)

The wind and waves instantly calmed. Experienced seamen and boaters know that in a storm, wind can suddenly stop, but the waves don't calm down for a long time. Someone watching this scene could have said, "Oh, it was just a coincidence that the wind suddenly stopped when Jesus stood and spoke," but it was certainly no coincidence that the water became instantly calm. It was a genuine miracle, and every person in the boat understood that fact.

In the storm, these twelve adults were as terrified as children. Several of them were skilled in handling a boat, but they weren't competent to face this problem. Actually, we can identify each element of resilience in this scene: The disciples were realistic about the danger—they were going to sink and maybe drown! They experienced Jesus right there in the boat with them (though he was asleep), and their only hope was that Jesus would come through. He intervened to rescue them, and in the surprising calm, they could look at their story and see both doubt and faith. When Jesus took over, they saw a better future: they saw the power of grace displayed, they were in it together, and they saw the triumph of Christ in the miracle.

The paradox of the Christian faith is that Jesus triumphed through suffering, and he won the greatest victory by his greatest sacrifice. His is an upside-down kingdom where the last shall be first and the first last, we rise by humbly bowing, and we gain power through serving.

> The paradox of the Christian faith is that Jesus triumphed through suffering, and he won the greatest victory by his greatest sacrifice.

We make a mistake when we equate political power with spiritual power, or worse, when we insist that spiritual power necessarily produces political power. In Jesus' kingdom, humility, kindness, justice, truth, and love are the hallmarks of its citizens. New Testament scholar N. T. Wright explains:

> Jesus doesn't give an explanation for the pain and sorrow of the world. He comes where the pain is most acute and takes it upon himself. Jesus doesn't explain why there is suffering, illness, and

death in the world. He brings healing and hope. He doesn't allow the problem of evil to be the subject of a seminar. He allows evil to do its worst to him. He exhausts it, drains its power, and emerges with new life.[38]

What does being triumphant in Christ look like? We could examine countless passages, but let's focus on one in Paul's letter to the Christians in Rome. After eleven chapters defining, explaining, and illustrating the power of the gospel message, he then turns to application. In a succinct trilogy that shows how a life of faith makes us resilient, he instructs them, "Rejoice in hope, be patient in tribulation, be constant in prayer" (Romans 12:12). In reverse order, the key words in these three phrases ("constant," "patient," and "rejoice") create the acronym, CPR . . . this is what keeps us spiritually, emotionally, and relationally alive! When we feel that we can't go on and when our hearts have stopped beating and we're oxygen-deprived, we need to stay connected to God in prayer, trusting that he knows, he cares, and he can do anything. We need to be realistic about enduring pain, trusting that God will use it for good if we let him. And when it appears that hope is gone, we cling to Jesus, knowing that sooner or later a new day is coming.

Constant in prayer

Jesus, the "breath of life," is oxygen for our souls, and prayer enables us to connect with him. We can survive forty days without food, four days without water, but only four minutes without oxygen. In other words, we need to practice getting spiritual oxygen through prayer so it becomes a regular, ingrained, vital part of our daily schedules. My daughter has a fish in a small aquarium. When she brought it home, it stayed on the kitchen countertop for a week or so, then she put it in the family room. She wanted to watch it at night when she went to bed, so she took it to her room, and finally, it found its permanent home in her bathroom. As long as the fish stayed in the aquarium, it didn't matter where she put it. The environment of the aquarium enabled the fish to thrive. Prayer is our aquarium. No matter where we go, what we do, or who we're with, a strong, intimate prayer life keeps us healthy and hopeful.

The object of our trust in times of comfort becomes our default source of hope in our moment of crisis. In other words, what we trust in the good times is all we've got when times are tough. Is Jesus our first response or our last resort? Is prayer a life-giving habit that provides joy and strength? If it is, it will sustain us when stress threatens to cripple us.

Patient in tribulation

Most of us aren't good at waiting. We want what we want, and we want it now! But throughout the Scriptures—and as we sit up and notice how our lives actually function—we see a lot of delays and detours. Waiting, though, isn't primarily about time—it's about our expectation. The phrase "wait on the Lord" or "wait for the Lord" doesn't mean we're just killing time. We anticipate his showing up and coming through . . . but always in his way and in his timing, which is almost never how we'd arrange the rescue!

The psalms are raw, honest prayers. In one of them, sung by pilgrims going to Jerusalem for one of the feasts, the writer cries out for God to "be attentive to the voice of my pleas for mercy!" What does the psalmist expect? What is his honest hope? He explains:

I wait for the Lord, my soul waits,
    and in his word I hope;
my soul waits for the Lord
    more than watchmen for the morning,
    more than watchmen for the morning. (Psalm 130:5-6)

Watchmen were soldiers who patrolled the ramparts of a city, looking for any signs of the enemy. Night was a time of particular anxiety because they couldn't see anyone sneaking up on the gates. They longed for the first rays of light. How certain were they that dawn would come? Absolutely certain. Their anxiety during the night was tempered with the certain expectation that the sun would come up the next morning. That's the picture the psalmist paints for himself and for us: as we wait, we can be certain that God will come through—perhaps through a long dark night, but eventually the light will reveal his hand at work.

Rejoicing in hope

It's very easy to be short-sighted and obsessed with the problems right in front of us. That's natural and normal, but it's spiritually deadly. We need binoculars to help us look backward and forward. We look back to remember the many times God has done what only he could do to provide, to protect, and to promote. We see how God turned tragedy into triumph, transforming waste places of doubt into gardens of renewed faith. And we see the people God has brought into our lives at just the right times to strengthen us, comfort us, and direct us.

But we also look forward—not just an hour, but an eon. The entire sweep of biblical history comes to an incredible consummation in the *palingenesia*, the renewal of all things in the new heavens and new earth. Then, all tears will be wiped away, pain will not even be a memory, and we'll dance and sing with our family and friends in the presence of God.

In a brilliant sermon during the darkest days for England in World War II, C. S. Lewis wanted to inject hope into the hearts of those who were in church that Sunday morning. He talked about the day when all wrongs would be made right, night will be turned into day, and heartache will be replaced with unvarnished joy. On that day, five things will happen: we'll be in the presence of Jesus, we'll be transformed to be like Jesus, we'll enjoy the greatest family feast the universe has ever known, we'll experience the amazing glory of being welcomed into the heart of God, and we'll be given roles in the celestial kingdom: "ruling cities, judging angels, being pillars of God's temple." To share God's glory, Lewis said, is unspeakable joy:

> It is written that we shall "stand before" Him, shall appear, shall be inspected. The promise of glory is the promise, almost incredible and only possible by the work of Christ, that some of us, that any of us who really chooses, shall actually survive that examination, shall find approval, shall please God. To please God . . . to be a real ingredient in the divine happiness . . . to be loved by God, not merely pitied, but delighted in as an artist delights in his work or a father in a son—it seems impossible, a weight or burden of glory which our thoughts can hardly sustain. But so it is.

When we let our imaginations scroll through the images of what this glory might be like for us, we're changed. The ultimate triumph of Christ transforms how we see ourselves and everyone around us. We realize that the reality of each person's eternal destiny—heaven or hell—gives us fresh eyes to see the people around us:

> It is a serious thing to live in a society of possible gods and goddesses, to remember that the dullest and most uninteresting person you talk to may one day be a creature which, if you saw it now, you would be strongly tempted to worship, or else a horror and a corruption such as you now meet, if at all, only in a nightmare. All day long we are, in some degree, helping each other to one or other of these destinations. It is in the light of these overwhelming possibilities, it is with the awe and the circumspection

proper to them, that we should conduct all our dealings with one another, all friendships, all loves, all play, all politics. There are no ordinary people. You have never talked to a mere mortal. Nations, cultures, arts, civilization—these are mortal, and their life is to ours as the life of a gnat. But it is immortals whom we joke with, work with, marry, snub, and exploit—immortal horrors or everlasting splendors.[39]

This our ultimate hope. This is how our hope changes our lives today.

THE RIGHT FOUNDATION

Resilience isn't just gritting our teeth and toughing out hard times. It's a different way of seeing, a new perspective, trusting that God is at work even when we can't see his hand moving at all. It's confidence that God is in control even though the world (or our lives at least) is coming apart at the seams. This view takes a radical reorientation, and it's far more about the heart than individual behaviors. Isaiah warned people they would become like their idols: dumb and lifeless. Today, I believe he would give the same warning: you'll become like your idols—superficial, wavering, and vanishing. When we love Jesus supremely, we become more like him . . . gradually, partially, but certainly. Far too often, the Christian life is depicted as a set of values and practices, but there's far more to it. As we've seen, the Scriptures tell us that God has "lavished" his grace on us in Christ, that we are his "treasures," the "apple of his eye." Our loves are

> When we love Jesus supremely, we become more like him . . . gradually, partially, but certainly.

shaped by our conception of God's love for us. If our love for him is lacking, it's certain that our grasp of his love for us is woefully small.

At the end of Jesus' most famous sermon, he summarizes by describing two roads, two gates, two trees, and two houses. We might assume he's contrasting good people and bad people, but I don't think that fits what he has said throughout the sermon. From the beginning he hasn't made the distinction between those who are good and those who are evil; his contrast is between those who are only religious and those who have a real connection with God, those who go through the motions and those who have a genuine heart for God.

The Pharisees were the most religious people in their culture, and they performed their spiritual rituals with great care, but their hearts were far from God. The elder brother in Jesus' story of the prodigal was dedicated and disciplined in his performance, but he didn't love his father or his brother. It's possible for people to be faithful members of a church, give and serve, but miss God in the process. Jesus told the crowd,

> "Not everyone who says to me, 'Lord, Lord,' will enter the kingdom of heaven, but the one who does the will of my Father who is in heaven. On that day many will say to me, 'Lord, Lord, did we not prophesy in your name, and cast out demons in your name, and do many mighty works in your name?' And then will I declare to them, 'I never knew you; depart from me, you workers of lawlessness.'" (Matthew 7:21-23)

Did you notice that these people called him "Lord, Lord"? In the Hebrew Scriptures, duplicate words signify intensity, like when David grieved for his slain son and wept, "Absalom, Absalom!" Here, people are crying out to God with passion, and they served in important roles, prophesying and doing "many mighty works" in God's name. But in a chilling statement, Jesus told them, "I never knew you. Depart from me."

Being religious, attending church, and using spiritual language may be an indication of genuine heart change and a vital relationship with Jesus, but it might not be. How can we know?

Jesus then told a parable about two houses. When the storm came, rain fell and winds blew the houses. Before the storm, the two houses looked identical, but something important was different: one had a foundation of sand, and it crumbled; the other was built on a rock, and it stood in the storm. The rock is Jesus and his teachings—not just hearing his words but obeying them.

Are you standing on that rock? Or are you standing on the shifting sand of religiosity, which shows up as being rules-oriented and critical of those who don't follow the rules? Or are you standing on the sand of self-indulgence, living for pleasure and comfort?

The cross is the only payment for our sins that enables us to be forgiven and free, and the resurrection is the source of life and power so we can live to please God. We triumph only through Christ. When I read the last part of Jesus' sermon, I remember scenes of my hometown on the west coast of Florida. The area has the highest incidents of hurricanes along the Atlantic and Gulf Coasts, so I have plenty of vivid memories of these storms. After particularly devastating hurricanes, streetlights hang limp, windows are shattered in office buildings, oak trees are uprooted, neighborhoods are devastated by flooding, and roofs have been blown off . . . but tall, stately palm trees continue to stand. They are a picture of resilience. Their roots have hung on tightly, their fronds have been whipped by fierce winds but have lasted, and though devastation is all around them, the palms remain as sentinels of hope that things will someday return to normal. The first psalm paints a picture of the resilience of a blessed person who has made a habit of making wise decisions and soaks in the truth of God's Word day and night. The psalmist says this person is like a strong, secure tree:

He is like a tree
>   planted by streams of water
> that yields its fruit in its season,
>   and its leaf does not wither.
> In all that he does, he prospers.
> The wicked are not so,
>   but are like chaff that the wind drives away. (Psalm 1:3-4)

When we walk with Christ, things don't return to normal after a time of suffering. We aren't like a rubber band that snaps back to its original shape after it has been stretched. We return, but we're different: wiser, stronger, more perceptive, and more resilient than before. Paul wasn't the same after suffering from his "thorn in his flesh." He asked God to take it away, but God had bigger and better plans. God spoke to Paul: "My grace is sufficient for you, for my power is made perfect in weakness." Paul responded, "Therefore I will boast all the more gladly of my weaknesses, so that the power of Christ may rest upon me. For the sake of Christ, then, I am content with weaknesses, insults, hardships, persecutions, and calamities. For when I am weak, then I am strong" (2 Corinthians 12:9-10).

When we trust God with our headaches and heartaches, we become more resilient, and our hearts are drawn closer to Jesus. We sense his love more fully, and we delight in his grace more than ever. We may do many of the same things we did before, but our motives have changed. John Newton was a slave trader who was saved and became a pastor. Later, he wrote "Amazing Grace" and many other beautiful hymns. In one of them, he describes the connection between a gospel-transformed heart and obedience:

> Our pleasure and our duty,
>   Though opposite before;
> Since we have seen his beauty,
>   Are joined to part no more.[40]

Isn't this what you want? Isn't this what you long for? Isn't this why you've read this book?

Sure it is. Me, too.

THE QUICKER GETTER-UPPER

I want to close the book with a story that inspires me. When Bonnie St. John was five years old, her right leg had to be amputated, but she found ways to pursue her dreams and developed incredible resilience. She took up the sport of snow skiing, and she was so good that she was favored to win the 1984 Winter Olympics in Innsbruck, Austria. The race consisted of two runs down the mountain. After the first one, Bonnie was in the lead. In the second, she fell, but she got up and completed her run. Her combined time earned a bronze medal for third place. Years later, Bonnie's zest for life and determined resilience resulted in her becoming a Harvard graduate, recipient of a Rhodes Scholarship, a mother, business owner, and an appointee by President Clinton to Director for Human Capital Issues on the White House National Economic Council. When she received the Fourth Annual John C. Maxwell Transformation Award, she told the story of her Olympic race. She talked about her two runs, and her fall, and she mentioned that the woman who won the gold medal also fell on one of her runs, but Bonnie explained, "She won the gold because she was the quicker getter-upper." She continued, "In life, people fall down, people get up. Be the quicker getter-upper and you will win the gold in life."[41]

That, in a nutshell, is the message of this book. We're going to fall, and sometimes we'll fall hard, maybe on the biggest stages of our lives. In those painful moments, it's easy to give up, but if we develop the discipline of getting up fast, we can take the next step and complete our bridge of resilience.

THINK ABOUT IT:

1. What are some comparisons and contrasts between a conquering Roman general and Jesus, our triumphant King?

2. How do you think you would have felt and reacted if you had been with the disciples in the storm while Jesus was asleep?

3. How would you have responded when he stood up and spoke, and the wind and waves calmed?

4. On a scale of 0 (none) to 10 (outstanding), rate yourself in how well you currently are:

    + Constant in prayer _____

    + Patient in tribulation _____

    + Rejoicing in hope _____

    What might need to improve in your grasp of God's love, grace, and purpose for you to grow stronger in these areas?

5. As you read this chapter, was there any indication that the Holy Spirit was whispering that your life is built on the shifting sand of self-righteousness? If so, pour out your heart to the Lord. If you relate to the elder brother in the story of the prodigal, you can pray something like this:

    Jesus, I've gone through the motions too long. Thank you for showing me that you love me dearly, and you died to free me from my self-righteousness. Thank you for your forgiveness. You are my Savior and my King, and I will follow you anywhere.

Or if you see yourself as a prodigal, self-indulgent and rebellious, you can pray:

Jesus, I've been so far from you, but you came after me. I've made a mess of my life, but you've forgiven me. Thank you for your love, your forgiveness, and the hope of a better tomorrow. Lead me, and I'll follow. I'm yours.

6. What are three things you've learned from this book? How will you apply those principles so you become more resilient in your faith, your relationships, and every other part of your life?

Affirmation:

We receive God's love by grace through faith, and God changes us from the inside out, so we want to obey the one who loves us so much.

ENDNOTES

1   Angela Duckworth, *Grit* (New York: Scribner, 2016), p. 192.

2   Ernest Shackleton, recounted in "Noble Oceans," http://www.nobleoceans.com/ideas-as-places/2017/7/3/ernest-shackleton-endurance

3   Frank Hurley, "The Stunning Survival Story of Ernest Shackleton and His Endurance Crew," *History*, https://www.history.com/news/shackleton-endurance-survival

4   A large body of research into resilience was begun a few decades ago and continues today. Some of the strategies taught in these articles are setting goals, challenging assumptions, regulating emotions, fighting through fear, seizing agency, and finding support. These tips are valuable, but they are, in my opinion, insufficient. The biblical framework of growing through suffering by depending on the wisdom, sovereignty, power, and grace of God is far stronger and more effective. (For instance, the American Psychological Association makes recommendations to those who want to build their resilience. See: https://www.apa.org/topics/resilience.)

5   "55 of Dr. Martin Luther King, Jr.'s Most Inspiring Motivational Quotes," *Parade*, January 17, 2021, https://parade.com/252644/viannguyen/15-of-martin-luther-king-jr-s-most-inspiring-motivational-quotes/

6   A. W. Tozer, edited by James L. Snyder, *Fellowship of the Burning Heart* (Alachua, FL: Bridge-Logos, 2006), p. 16.

7   J. I. Packer, *Knowing God* (Downers Grove, Illinois: InterVarsity Press, 1973), pp. 226-228.

8   Tim Keller, *Walking with God through Pain and Suffering* (New York: Riverhead Books, 2013), p. 5.

9   Walter Ciszek, *He Leadeth Me*, (San Francisco: Ignatius, 1973), pp. 38, 142, 175, 182, 57, 79.

10 Philip Yancey, *Reaching for the Invisible God* (Grand Rapids: Zondervan, 2000), p. 69.

11 Bill Keller, "Nelson Mandela, South Africa's Liberator as Prisoner and President, Dies at 95," *New York Times*, December 6, 2013, https://www.nytimes.com/2013/12/06/world/africa/nelson-mandela_obit.html

12 "Hunger in America," https://www.feedingamerica.org/hunger-in-america

13   Statistics compiled by The Center for Family Justice, https://centerforfamilyjustice.org/community-education/statistics/

14   Kim Parker, Rachel Minkin, and Jesse Bennett, "Economic Fallout from COVID-19 Continues to Hit Lower-Income Americans the Hardest," Pew Research Center, September 24, 2020, https://www.pewresearch.org/social-trends/2020/09/24/economic-fallout-from-covid-19-continues-to-hit-lower-income-americans-the-hardest/

15   W. David O. Taylor, "Psalms of Justice," The Gospel Coalition, June 16, 2020, https://www.thegospelcoalition.org/article/psalms-of-justice/

16   Miroslav Volf, *Exclusion and Embrace* (Nashville: Abingdon Press, 2019), p. 300.

17   Nelson Mandela, *Long Walk to Freedom* (New York: Little, Brown & Co., 2008), cited in the foreword.

18   Lewis Smedes, *Forgive and Forget* (New York: Harper & Row, 1984), pp. 79-80.

19   Lewis Smedes, *The Art of Forgiving: When You Need to Forgive and Don't Know How* (New York: Ballantine Books, 1996), p. 171.

20   Joni Eareckson, *Joni* (Grand Rapids: Zondervan, 1976), pp. 13-14.

21   "Joni Eareckson Tada Shares Her Story," YouTube, January 28, 2014, https://www.youtube.com/watch?v=VVXJ8GyLgt0

22   Tim Keller, *King's Cross* (New York: Dutton, 2011), pp. 98-99.

23   Malcolm Gladwell, *David and Goliath* (New York: Hachett Book Group, 2013), p. 5.

24   Ron Carucci, "The Better You Know Yourself, the More Resilient You'll Be," *Harvard Business Review*, September 4, 2017, https://hbr.org/2017/09/the-better-you-know-yourself-the-more-resilient-youll-be

25   Vera Tobin, "The Science of the Plot Twist: How Writers Exploit Our Brains," The Conversation, May 11, 2018, https://theconversation.com/the-science-of-the-plot-twist-how-writers-exploit-our-brains-95748

26   "Developing Resilience," https://www.mindtools.com/pages/article/resilience.htm

27   Brené Brown, *The Gifts of Imperfection* (Center City, Minnesota: Hazelden, 2010), p. 25.

28   Adapted from *The Complete Works of Stephen Charnock, Volume 4* (Oxford University Press, 1865), p. 199.

29   Martin Luther's "95 Theses," https://www.luther.de/en/95thesen.html

30   Christian Smith and Melinda Denton, *Soul Searching: The Religious and Spiritual Lives of American Teenagers*, National Study of Youth and Religion (Notre Dame, Indiana: University of Notre Dame), pp. 162-163.

31   Larry Crabb, *Finding God*, (Grand Rapids: Zondervan, 1993), p. 18.

32   "Social Media Fact Sheet," Pew Research Center, June 12, 2019, https://www.pewresearch.org/internet/fact-sheet/social-media/

33   Studies cited by Marisa T. Cohen, Ph.D., in "Social Media and Relationships," *Psychology Today*, December 4, 2018, https://www.psychologytoday.com/us/blog/finding-love-the-scientific-take/201812/social-media-and-relationships

34   "More Than Eight-in-Ten Americans Get News from Digital Platforms," Pew Research Center, January 12, 2021, www.pewresearch.org

35   "Kalev Leetaru, "Is Social Media Curating Hate and Scouring the Web for Our Greatest Fears?" *Forbes*, May 13, 2019, https://www.forbes.com/sites/kalevleetaru/2019/05/13/is-social-media-curating-hate-and-scouring-the-web-for-our-greatest-fears/?sh=7bb648de4cf3

36   Les and Leslie Parrott, *Real Relationships* (Grand Rapids: Zondervan, 1998), p. 11.

37   Lucian of Samosata, *The Passing of Peregrinus*, cited at https://reformedwiki.com/lucian-of-samosata-and-jesus-existence

38   N. T. Wright, "Deconstructing the Bully God," February 13, 2015, www.patheos.com

39   C. S. Lewis, "The Weight of Glory," a sermon preached in the Church of St. Mary the Virgin, Oxford, England, June 8, 1942, https://www.wheelersburg.net/Downloads/Lewis%20Glory.pdf

40   John Newton, Hymn 3, Proverbs 3:17, https://www.ccel.org/ccel/newton/olney-hymns.Book3.invit.h3_3.html

41   Diana Wood, "Transform Your Life . . . with Diana Wood: Win the gold medal in your life by being 'the quicker getter-upper,'" Morgan Hill Life, September 27-October 10, 2017, https://morganhilllife.com/2017/10/16/transform-your-life-with-diana-wood-win-the-gold-medal-in-your-life-by-being-the-quicker-getter-upper/

ACKNOWLEDGMENTS

As the author, my name is on the cover of this book, but I'm the first to admit that the message in these pages is the product of many who have had a profound impact on my life. I could list many people, but I want to focus on a few. I want to thank . . .

Dr. J. E. Hightower, the former Pastor of Elizabeth Baptist Church.

Dr. Hightower was one of the quintessential exemplars of resilience that I've known. He faithfully proclaimed the Word of God for seventy years, pastored the people of God for sixty-seven years, and lived resiliently for ninety-eight years until taking his well-deserved rest. It is my great honor to be his son in the faith as I strive to uphold the spiritual foundation he established. I hope I make him proud.

The staff and the people of Elizabeth Baptist Church.

In the many years we've served together, I've often marveled at your love for God, your steadfast commitment to his calling, and your tender hearts for the people he brings to us. Through the joys and heartaches of life, I've been inspired by your resilience to keep following God every day.

Craig, Jr., Corrie, and Charlee, my trinity of love.

It is my greatest joy and honor to be your dad. There has not been a day since each of you entered this world that I've gone without praying for your resilience as you face this beautiful and exciting (but too often ruthless) world. You are pioneers on your own unique journeys to greatness. As a family, we're building bridges, not walls . . . a bridge of resilience.

Cleo, *my beloved wife.*

Your love still captures and consumes my heart. Thank you for the grace, support, and patience you've given me as my lifelong companion. Together, we share our journey in this sacred calling to serve God's people. You bring extraordinary balance to our home and blessings to our hearts. You radiate with resilience. I don't know where I'd be without you.

USING *RESILIENT* IN SMALL GROUPS AND CLASSES

Resilient is designed for individual study, small groups, and classes. The best way to absorb and apply these principles is for each person to individually study and answer the questions at the end of each chapter, and then discuss them in a group environment.

Order enough copies of the book for each person to have a copy. For couples, encourage both to have their own book so they can record their individual reflections.

A recommended schedule for a small group or class might be:

Week 1

Introduce the material. As a group leader, tell your story of experiencing meaningful relationships, share your hopes for the group, and provide books for each person. Encourage people to read the assigned chapter each week and answer the questions.

Weeks 2–10

Each week, introduce the topic for the week and share a story of how God has used the principles in your life. Lead people through a discussion of the questions at the end of the chapter.

Personalize Each Lesson

Don't feel pressured to cover every question in your group discussions. Pick out three or four that had the biggest impact on you, and focus on those, or ask people in the group to share their responses to the questions that meant the most to them that week.

Make sure you personalize the principles and applications. At least once in each group meeting, add your own story to illustrate a particular point.

Make the Scriptures come alive. Far too often, we read the Bible like it's a phone book, with little or no emotion. Paint a vivid picture for people. Provide insights about the risk and the power of authentic relationships, and help those in your group sense the emotions of specific people in each scene.

Focus on Application

The questions at the end of each chapter and your encouragement to group members to be authentic will help your group take big steps to apply the principles they're learning. Share how you are applying the principles in particular chapters each week, and encourage them to take steps of growth, too.

Three Types of Questions

If you've led groups for a few years, you already understand the importance of using open questions to stimulate discussion. Three types of questions are *limiting, leading,* and *open.* Many of the questions at the end of each lesson are open questions.

Limiting questions focus on an obvious answer, such as, "What does Jesus call himself in John 10:11?" They don't stimulate reflection or discussion. If you want to use questions like these, follow them with thought-provoking, open questions.

Leading questions require the listener to guess what the leader has in mind, such as, "Why did Jesus use the metaphor of a shepherd in John 10?" (He was probably alluding to a passage in Ezekiel, but many people don't know that.) The teacher who asks a leading question has a definite answer in mind. Instead of asking this kind of question, you should just teach the point and perhaps ask an open question about the point you have made.

Open questions usually don't have right or wrong answers. They stimulate thinking, and they are far less threatening because the person answering doesn't risk ridicule for being wrong. These questions often begin with "Why do you think . . .?" or "What are some reasons that . . .?" or "How would you have felt in that situation?"

Preparation

As you prepare to teach this material in a group, consider these steps:

1. Carefully and thoughtfully read the book. Make notes, highlight key sections, quotes, or stories, and complete the reflection section at the end of each chapter. This will familiarize you with the entire scope of the content.

2. As you prepare for each week's group, read the corresponding chapter again and make additional notes.

3. Tailor the amount of content to the time allotted. You may not have time to cover all the questions, so pick the ones that are most pertinent.

4. Add your own stories to personalize the message and add impact.

5. Before and during your preparation, ask God to give you wisdom, clarity, and power. Trust him to use your group to change people's lives.

6. Most people will get far more out of the group if they read the chapter and complete the reflection each week. Order books before the group or class begins or after the first week.

ABOUT THE AUTHOR

As Senior Pastor of Elizabeth Baptist Church, Craig L. Oliver, Sr. synthesizes Bible-based preaching with cultural relevance and God-inspired passion to effect transformation in the hearts and minds of his global audience. He has seen the providential hand of God increase his influence since becoming the pastor of Elizabeth Baptist Church, expanding the membership to close to 10,000 members and evolving to a multisite ministry model with five campuses throughout Metro Atlanta, Georgia. Craig's ministry truly exemplifies the Apostle Paul's connection between the inward experience of grace and our outward expression of it in Ephesians 2:10: "For we are his workmanship, created in Christ Jesus unto good works, which God hath before ordained that we should walk in them."

Serving as EBC's Senior Pastor for nearly thirty years, Craig has positioned himself as a beacon of spiritual guidance, cutting-edge leadership expertise, and community activism. He is a man with a passion for his community, engaging in philanthropic work in partnership with local and regional municipalities and is a proud member of the Omega Psi Phi fraternity. An avid reader with an insatiable thirst for knowledge, Craig endeavors to shape his community with the wisdom he has gleaned as a lifelong student of the Bible and life.

Beyond having a heart for the local and regional community, Craig has a great passion for the global arena. He has eagerly engaged in mission work and preaching in Africa, Asia, India, and Jamaica, extending the breadth of his reach to international proportions. His practical message of hope is firmly rooted in the unadulterated truth of the Scriptures, and he passionately communicates the love of Jesus Christ to people around the world.

This dynamic author relishes traveling, enjoys fishing, loves dogs, and is an all-around outdoorsman. He has received a myriad of accolades and degrees, including a Master of Arts degree in Biblical/Theological Studies and Leadership from Luther Rice Theological Seminary and a D.Min. from Gordon Conwell Theological Seminary. He is presently pursuing a Ph.D. in Organizational Leadership from Anderson University. Though

greatly accomplished in ministry, academia, and philanthropy, the center of his heart is his family. Craig and his wife, Chi'Ira, have three beautiful children: son Craig Jr., and daughters Corrie Kené and Charlee Reign. Craig recognizes his family as not only the perfect balance in his life, but also as the greatest expression of his success.

RESOURCES

To order more copies of this book, go to

CraigLOliverMinistries.com